MAX
MOMENTS

MAX
MOMENTS

POWERFUL LESSONS TO
HELP YOU BREAK THROUGH FROM
GOOD TO GREAT

MAX ROOKE

Dedicated to those who believe the best is yet to come.

"Life is found in the dance between your
deepest desire and your greatest fear."

TONY ROBBINS

TABLE OF CONTENTS

BONUS SECTION 213
MAX MOMENTS ON THE JOURNEY

INTRODUCTION

What you have here in this book is a series of short stories called "Max Moments."

What is a Max Moment? A Max Moment is a short lesson that provides you with an opportunity to gain a powerful insight. An insight is simply a moment in life when everything changes. It is a moment when you stop and look at things in a different way. It is a moment when the ordinary becomes extraordinary. It is a moment when the impossible becomes possible. And all it takes is one insight to change your life!

I know this because I have had the privilege of working in the world of high performance for over twenty years. I have spent my life studying why people do what they do and what the very best do differently than everyone else. I have worked and consulted with some of the best including NCAA All-Americans, professional athletes,

Olympic medalists, hall of fame coaches, and national champions, and I have seen first-hand what makes them great. One of the biggest things I have learned from working with top performers is this: what got you to where you are today, won't get you to where you want to be tomorrow. Reaching the next level requires a very different way of thinking than all the previous levels. This book is going to uncover some of the invisible forces that are currently holding you back and challenge you to think in a different way...

One of the ways it will challenge you is to help you become a "master of meaning" in your life. Everything that happens in life, we must give meaning to. The meaning we associate to each event determines how we view the event, how we feel about the event, and what actions we are willing to take because of the event. This is the reason why two people can experience the same event and have completely different reactions based on the meaning they give to it. For instance, let's imagine that two people experience the same setback in life. Person A might focus on all the reasons why this is a negative. Because of these reasons they associate a meaning of limitation that holds them back, creating an "I can't" attitude. In turn this negative meaning leads to the action of giving up. Now person B has a different approach. Instead, they focus on all the reasons why this same problem could be a positive in their life. They look at things differently and instead ask:

- ➔ What if this setback is actually life's way of helping me and not hurting me?

- ➔ What if this problem was truly a gift?

- ➔ What if this obstacle was not the end but just the beginning?

Because of these reasons they associate a new meaning of empowerment that lifts them up, creating an "I can" attitude. This alternative meaning leads them to the action of not giving up and overcoming the obstacle they faced. Same event, two different outcomes. The only difference was the meaning given to the event.

For me personally, my life changed when I changed the meanings I associated with the events that happened in my life. Since then I have been able to create the kind of life I only dreamed about and help others to do the same. The success, joy, and abundance I get to experience daily is beyond anything I could have imagined and I want the same to happen for you. It will happen when you start thinking in a different way. That is what these Max Moments are designed to do. To challenge you to think differently and seek new meanings for the events that happen in your life. If you can master meaning, you can master your life!

Lastly, let me explain how to read this book so you can get the most out of it. Each one of these Max Moments will deliver a powerful message to create new meanings you can apply to your life. To help you apply it, there will be some action questions at the end of each Max Moment for you to answer. I encourage you to take the time to think about and write down your answers before moving on to the next Max Moment. You will thank yourself later!

Collectively, all these Max Moments address five key areas that determine the level at which you will choose to play the game of life: your vision, your mindset, your habits, your resilience, and your happiness.

>**Vision:** To create the life you want, you must first create the vision in your mind. You must know where you are going because without a vision, people perish.

>**Mindset:** Building a positive mindset is vital to support your vision. With the right mindset, you can accomplish anything you want in life.

Habits: To support your vision and mindset, you must have strong habits. Taking action moves you forward in life, which requires great habits.

Resilience: It is not a matter of if adversity is going to happen to you, rather a matter of when. When it does, you must meet it with a level of resilience that will allow you to continue on your journey toward what you want.

Happiness: It is vitally important to always live with an attitude of gratitude. This will increase your level of happiness and help you enjoy the process of achieving levels of greatness even more!

Ultimately, my intention is that these Max Moments help you to see something in yourself that you may not have seen before, which will then help you break through from good to GREAT!

Enjoy, and as always choose to Live Life 2 The Max!

MAX MOMENTS ON VISION

THE $12,000 PIZZA

How much would you pay for a pizza?

$10 for one you throw in a microwave.

Maybe $20 at a restaurant.

How about $40 if it was a massive pizza?

What about if it was the pizza to end all pizzas, topped with the world's finest foods sourced from all over the world? Would you pay $100, $500... Try $12,000!

Yes, that's right, the Louis XIII is the most expensive pizza in the world and costs $12,000.

Do people buy it? Absolutely...

Now, you have to live in Italy to make an order. But when you do, the master chef comes to your house and cooks this amazing treat for you using the finest ingredients on the planet like lobster, Mediterranean squid, caviar, and a very rare sea salt. Ingredients like this make it a little different to Papa John's or Pizza Hut! But here is the thing, why do people buy it? The answer is because it is the ONLY pizza like it in the world! It is a truly special experience and people treat it that way.

So, why am I talking about a $12,000 pizza when it comes to your personal development and the vision you have for your life? Because you are the only person in the world like you. You are truly something special with a unique passion and purpose only you can fulfill. And you need to treat it that way. Yet, I see a lot of people treat their lives and what they are capable of like a $10 microwave pizza or half-eaten takeaway pizza, left on the table, and tossed in the rubbish like nobody cares. If you are being really honest with yourself, have you thought this way before? And if this has been you, is that honestly the life you were destined to lead? Deep down you know the answer is that you are destined for something more, something greater, and something truly special, even if you sometimes doubt yourself or choose not to believe it.

Just like the $12,000 pizza is the BEST pizza in the world, you deserve to lead your BEST life. That will all start when you realize how unique you are, and it will start when you realize that you are the ONLY person in the world who can do what you do!

So I will leave you with this question from Buckminster Fuller about having a vision for your life which drives home the importance of just how special each of our lives are. He asks this:

> "What is my job on the planet? What is it that needs doing, that I know something about, that probably won't happen unless I take responsibility for it?"

Now apply it to your life and think about what needs doing that probably won't happen unless you take responsibility for it. Just like the Italian pizza chefs, show up to make a $12,000 pizza that no one else can make. I wrote this book because I believe that part of my responsibility is to remind you of the greatness that lies within you, because if not you, then who?

ACTION QUESTIONS

➜ **What needs doing that probably won't happen unless you take responsibility for it?**

GET A BIGGER FRYING PAN

There was a boy who was out fishing at a pond one day and he was having such a great time and catching a lot of fish. There was an older gentleman who was on the other side of the pond who was watching this boy fish. As he was watching, he would see the boy catch a fish, pull it out of the water, and then hold it up to assess it. If it was a small fish, the boy would keep it and if it was a big fish, he would throw it back into the water. The gentleman watched the boy repeat this process again and again for about an hour and couldn't understand why he was doing it.

So finally the gentleman walked around the pond to the boy and said, "Hi, how are you doing?" The boy said, "Oh I am doing great, thank you and I am catching a ton of fish". The gentleman said "Ahh, wonderful to hear. But

I noticed you seem to be keeping all the small fish you catch and throw the big ones back in the pond. That seems a little strange, so might I ask why you do that, because usually it's the other way around?" The boy looked at him and said, "Oh yes sir, that's very easy. I only have a seven-inch frying pan!"

Think about that for a moment...

Many people limit what is possible in their lives because they only have a seven-inch frying pan (they only have a small vision). The limited size of their frying pan means they can never break through to the next level and generate anything bigger than the world they created for themselves within that small frying pan.

So the key takeaway here is this: get a bigger frying pan!

Get a bigger world, get bigger dreams, get bigger goals, get around bigger people, go have bigger experiences, go after bigger opportunities and play a bigger game. To do that, you need to get bigger expectations, a bigger vision, and a bigger frying pan! Because we get what we EXPECT in life. If the boy had a bigger frying pan, he would have had bigger expectations and thus would have kept some of the bigger fish. The same is true of you. You will get what you expect in life.

Having said this, many people's expectations for their life lower over time, preventing them from playing a bigger game. Their expectations shrink because of all the tough things they have suffered in life, the adversity they have gone through, the many times they have been told no, the constant feeling of not being good enough, or all the curve balls life has thrown at them. At some point, they lose that sense of wonder and expectation. When we lose our sense of curiosity and expectation, it limits our vision and extinguishes all the great things we can attract into our life. Why?

Because we only have a seven-inch frying pan...

So my advice to you: Get A Bigger Frying Pan!

ACTION QUESTIONS

→ **How are you currently limiting what's possible in your life because you only have a seven-inch frying pan?**

→ **What would getting a bigger frying pan help you to do, create, and achieve in your life?**

HOMING INSTINCT

I have something really remarkable I want to share with you about bird instincts.

Birds have an incredible sense of direction called a homing instinct, which allows them to find and return to the same place year after year, even if their migration takes them halfway around the world thousands of miles away from home. How this feat is accomplished has been the subject of many studies.

For instance, there have been extensive studies done on homing pigeons. They were tagged and transported to various places around the world and then released to see whether they could find their way home. In one study the birds were transported in a closed box from the coast of Great Britain and flown all the way to Boston, Massachusetts. Remarkably, when the birds were released from the closed box, they flew thousands of miles across the

Atlantic Ocean and found their way back home to their nest in 12 days and 12 hours!

People are amazed by this inbuilt homing instinct capacity, which is basically the ability to find their way home across great distances despite unfamiliar environments. All the research indicates that they have an internal compass or an internal map that they can rely on even if they don't know where they are!

Pretty impressive, right?

Well, I believe that there is a similar homing instinct hard-wired into all of us, and it's called our PURPOSE. At our very core, as humans, we seek purpose. We seek to connect with and believe in, a cause greater and more enduring than ourselves. That drive comes from a place within, where intrinsic motivation (internal rewards) is valued higher than extrinsic motivation (external rewards). Those that harness the power of purpose will always hold that innate ability, like the birds, to find their way home to what really matters most, no matter the distance or unfamiliar environments.

For instance, research from Johns Hopkins University showed that when people were asked what they considered "Very Important": 16% said making a lot of money (extrinsic motivation) and 78% said finding a meaning and purpose to life (intrinsic motivation).

So, what am I saying? I am saying when things get tough for you, when you feel in an unfamiliar place, when life is difficult to make sense of, and when you are not sure which direction to go in your life, remember this: you have a homing instinct with an internal compass and map to guide you. It's called your PURPOSE.

To activate your purpose, begin with asking WHY?

Because it was Nietzsche who said: "He who has a WHY to live for can bear almost any how."

ACTION QUESTIONS

On the following page is a series of thought-provoking questions to use your homing instinct and help guide you to what really matters most...

Here are four WHY questions about PURPOSE:

WHY?

→ Why go for it?

→ Why sacrifice so much?

→ Why put yourself out there?

WHY NOT?

→ Why not see how far you can go?

→ Why not see what is waiting for you on the other side of your problems?

→ Why not go all-in?

WHY NOT YOU?

→ If it has happened for others, why not you?

→ If it has never been done before, why not you?

→ If others say it is impossible, why not you?

WHY NOW?

→ When is a better time than right now to make your dreams a reality?

→ Why not hit the next level of success, happiness and fulfillment you want right now?

→ Why not be the person you have always wanted to be today?

ONE
MARSHMALLOW
OR TWO

What I am about to share with you is one of the most important characteristics in determining a person's success in life and it is probably not what you think!

In 1960, Walter Mischel, who was a professor at Stanford, began an important psychological study. He tested hundreds of children around the age of four or five by putting them into a private room and sitting them down in a chair. He placed a single marshmallow on the table in front of them.

The child was offered a deal...

The adult researcher said they were going to leave the room and if the child did not eat the marshmallow while they were away, then the child would be rewarded with a second marshmallow when the researcher came back. However, if the child decided to eat the first marshmallow before the researcher came back, then they would not get the second marshmallow. Makes sense so far. What is also important to note is the child did not know how long they would have to wait before the researcher came back, but it was usually about 15 minutes.

So the choice was simple: one marshmallow treat right now or two marshmallow treats later?

As you can imagine, for young kids ages four or five, it took every ounce of effort and strength to not eat that yummy marshmallow in front of them. Now, for some of the children, they just caved under the pressure and ate the marshmallow, while others were able to sit there and wait the entire time.

But here is the most interesting part of the entire study. Years later the researchers did a follow-up study to track the children's progress as they became adults and this is what they found: the children who were willing to delay gratification and wait to receive the second marshmallow were more successful in many areas of life as adults. Crazy, right?

So this study makes one thing very clear. Your ability to succeed at anything you want in life will largely be dependent on your ability to use the power of delayed gratification, which means being disciplined enough to do what is right, not what is easy.

Now I am not saying that one choice made at four years old is going to determine the rest of your life. But what I am saying is that this marshmallow experiment can be a great reminder to us all that in a world dominated by the desire for instant gratification, what can lead us to the success and happiness we desire in life is actually the opposite: delayed gratification.

ACTION QUESTIONS

➔ **What is something big you want in life that you can apply the concept of delayed gratification to. How can delayed gratification help you stay connected to that vision and not give up?**

THE RICHEST PLACE IN THE WORLD

Where is the richest place in the world?

Most people automatically think of countries such as Qatar, Luxembourg, Singapore, Brunei, and other seemingly glamorous places. But when I researched the answer to this question, the result I got changed everything for me. It was speaker Les Brown who explained the actual answer to this question:

> "The graveyard is the richest place on earth,
> because it is here that you will find all the
> hopes and dreams that were never fulfilled,
> the books that were never written, the songs
> that were never sung, the inventions that were

never shared, the cures that were never discovered. All because someone was too afraid to
take that first step or keep with the problem or
determined to carry out their dream."

Reading this, I immediately began to assess my current
life, my daily actions, my relationships, and whether
I was making use of the God-given gifts I have been
blessed with. I ask you the same question. Are you truly
living and sharing all of your talents, ideas, abilities, and
love? Are you making the most of every opportunity?

If the answer is no, the main reason you are not living to
your full potential is because of FEAR. The fear of failure:
what if you try and things don't work out? And just as
paralyzing is the fear of success: what if things do work
out and you can't handle it?

In our lives, we will not regret taking action and failing
because failure is a part of life and the process toward
achievement. However, what we will regret is the fear
of taking no action at all. What can we do to overcome
this fear and not take our riches to the graveyard? We
must realize we have something very special to give to
the world, and thus we have a responsibility to share it.
We must decide to take the first step toward our dream.
Decide to step away from all that has been holding us

back, decide not to quit when things get tough, decide to connect with people who will stretch us and push us, decide to truly listen to our heart, decide to love without fear of being hurt, decide to live with faith, and decide today to be the person God made us to be.

We get one opportunity at life, and with each passing moment we will never get it back. Author Mark Batterson wrote: "I refuse to believe that the purpose of life is to arrive at death safely." I agree with him. The purpose of life is not to get to the end safely and then realize you could have done more. The purpose of life is to share the unique gifts you have been blessed with to make your impact on the world.

Everything will change in your life when you shift your mindset from thinking less about what you expect from life to one where you think more about what life expects from you!

ACTION QUESTIONS

→ **What unique gifts have you been blessed with and how can you use them to make an impact in the world?**

WHERE'S WALLY

Let me guess, you have way too many things to do and not enough time to do them.

Your TO DO list just keeps getting longer and longer and the days seem to get shorter and shorter because you can't find time to fit everything in...

Even worse is how it affects your physical, mental, and emotional state. You get bogged down in all the things you feel you HAVE to do, which creates feelings of stress, anxiety and overwhelm. This causes you to slip away from what matters most because you can't see through the cloud of busyness that's right in front of your face.

So what do you crave more of? TIME.

But it is not possible to get more time because we all get the same 24 hours in a day, nothing more and nothing less.

Does that sound like you?

If it does, you are not alone…

You see, this dilemma of how most people choose to live day-to-day reminds me of a famous children's puzzle book that was originally published back in 1987 by Martin Handford called *Where's Wally* (or *Where's Waldo* in the US). Check this out, there have been over 58 million *Where's Wally* books sold!

If you remember, the book consisted of a series of illustrations with hundreds, and sometimes thousands, of people doing a variety of things inside the picture. The reader was then challenged to find Wally, who was hidden somewhere in that picture. Now Wally always wore the same thing and could be identified by his distinctive red and white striped shirt, bobble hat, and glasses. But here is the thing, no matter how well you know Wally and what you are looking for, it is always extremely difficult to locate him in the picture, and the reason is that there are so many other things vying for your attention so your focus gets distracted.

Now the same is true of you, isn't it? There are so many things vying for your attention each day that you probably get stuck on all the things you feel you should do, and do not leave yourself enough time for the most important things: what you must do. Am I right?

So imagine for a moment that your life was one of the *Where's Wally* illustrations. Now imagine that Wally represented the most important things in your life. How easy would it be for you to find him amongst everything else you have going on?

I imagine it's pretty tough...

So, if you can't get more time, how can you make it easier to find Wally in your life?

You must remove all the clutter, all the excess, and all the craziness from your life and start prioritizing and focusing on what really matters most to you.

The *Where's Wally* books would say that Wally was always on his FANTASTIC JOURNEY. I want to remind you that you deserve to have your own FANTASTIC JOURNEY in your life. But to have it, you first must be able to find it!

After reading this, I encourage you to find a *Where's Wally* picture so you can see what I am talking about.

ACTION QUESTIONS

Get a piece of paper and draw a line down the middle.

➜ In the left column, make a list to answer this question: what things (clutter, excess, busyness, craziness) do you need to remove to help you focus on what matters most?

➜ In the right column, make a list to answer these questions: what things (Wally) matter most to you? What do you need to start prioritizing and focusing on?

THE KARMAN LINE

"When you reach for the stars, you are reaching for the farthest thing out there. When you reach deep into yourself, it is the same thing, but in the opposite direction. If you reach in both directions, you will have spanned the universe."

VERA NAZARIAN

Do you remember being told "shoot for the stars" when referring to your dreams and hopes? Well, the closest star to us is the sun, which is about 93 million miles from earth and gravity is keeping us from getting there! Gravitational pull is an invisible force that causes objects to pull other objects towards them. For instance, when a person jumps up in the air, it is the earth's gravitational pull that causes them to return to the ground.

I look at our lives in the same way. We all grow up wanting to shoot for the stars with big dreams and goals we want to achieve. But throughout life we experience adversity and other obstacles that get in the way, and, like gravity, it creates invisible forces such as fear and doubt that drag us down. So we never reach the heights we know we are capable of.

But there is a point in the atmosphere where this changes, it is called "The Karman Line." Named after the Hungarian-American engineer and physicist Theodore von Karman, the Karman Line is 100 kilometers/62 miles above sea level. It commonly represents the imaginary boundary between the earth's atmosphere and outer space. In theory, once this line is crossed, the air becomes so thin that gravity does not have the same effect.

But making it to the Karman Line is the hardest part of the entire trip. For instance, a spaceship spends more energy getting out of the atmosphere than it does on the rest of the entire journey.

In this way, our lives are just like space travel. As T.F. Hodge said, "the sky is not my limit. I am."

The first step toward positive change is always the hardest. Creating change takes a lot of willpower, energy, and persistence initially. But instead of succumbing to the invisible forces, like gravity, wanting to pull us back down, we must remain faithful and courageous in the pursuit of our dreams. While we often use circumstances as excuses for why we fail, the gravity holding us back in life is really our inability to get out of our own way and believe that we are the masters of our own destiny.

When you break free of that pattern, you will have the power of a rocket launcher to reach for your own personal Karman Line. When you reach it, you will be set free to live and explore an extraordinary life that is physically, mentally, and emotionally out of this world!

ACTION QUESTIONS

There is a tradition in NASA that special astronaut badges are awarded to anyone who flies above the Karman Line. So my question to you is this:

➜ **When and how are you going to earn your astronaut badge for living a life worthy of being above the Karman Line?**

PERIOD VS. COMMA

Writing is an integral part of our lives and knowing how to express yourself through the written word can be a powerful tool.

Now, while it is hard to say exactly how many words there are in the English language, the Oxford English Dictionary contains just over 170,000 full entries. In addition, there are fourteen punctuation marks commonly used in English grammar, and the two most commonly used punctuation marks are the period and the comma. I want to talk about how they affect our daily lives.

In written terms, a period is a punctuation mark placed at the end of a sentence to show it has finished. A comma is a punctuation mark that indicates a brief pause in a sentence but is not as final as a period. Now, if you use either of these punctuation marks in the wrong way, it will not make sense to the reader. Apply this concept to your life and ask yourself this: have you ever placed a period in your life when all you needed was a comma?

Just as a punctuation mark defines the course of a sentence, the punctuation marks we use at critical moments in our lives will determine our course and trajectory. I see too many people face adversity and setbacks, then choose to put a period instead of a comma. For instance, after getting knocked down, being told no, or losing, we make these struggles finite by placing a period after it and concluding that the vision we have and what we want for our lives is no longer possible.

- What if Thomas Edison had put a PERIOD after his thousands of failed attempts at making the incandescent lightbulb.

- What if Walt Disney had put a PERIOD after being told he "lacked creativity."

- What if the Beatles had put a PERIOD after being told they had "no future in show business."

- What if Beethoven had put a PERIOD after becoming deaf.

- What if Abraham Lincoln had put a PERIOD after multiple failures at running for office.

Like these amazing role models, if we decided to place a comma in our most important decisions, we would see failure not as the end, but as the next part of our process. We would see setbacks as a setup for something even greater. This perspective is an incredibly powerful tool. Because when we have a growth mindset, we can begin to see everything that happens in our lives as an opportunity to learn and grow, even the pain, the rejections, the failures, the losses, and the suffering.

So, the big question you need to ask yourself is: which story are you going to tell yourself?

Will it be a story of disappointment or a story of triumph that you tell for the rest of your life?

And that story depends on whether you choose to use a period or a comma!

Let me say this. The level of success you will achieve in your life depends on your ability to overcome adversity and delay gratification. Thus, in the most important areas of your life, you must remove the period and replace it with a comma. Just stay the course, stay connected to your purpose, don't give up on your vision, and believe in a brighter tomorrow because I am telling you: the best is yet to come.

So when it comes to the vision and purpose you have for your life, remember what author Mark Houlahan said, "If you want your life to be a magnificent story, then begin by realizing that you are the author and every day you have the opportunity to write a new page."

ACTION QUESTIONS

In the story of your life you have written thus far:

→ What areas have you placed a period?

→ What has it prevented you from doing, being, and creating?

→ What would happen if you placed a comma there instead?

→ What would it open up for you to do, be, and create?

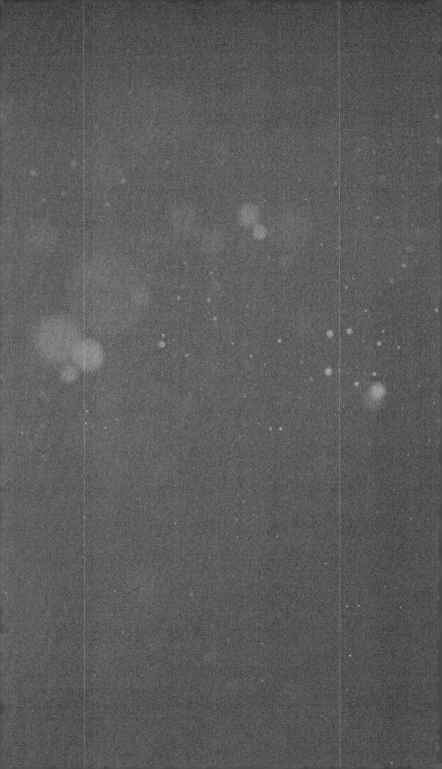

MAX MOMENTS ON MINDSET

A OR B

There was a real study set up in a medical school for people who were training to be surgeons who were getting ready to take their final examination before certification. The professor came into the room for the three hour exam and, to the surprise of all the students, gave them one of two choices.

The first option was the opportunity for the students to get a B grade without having to take the test. The second option was for the students to remain in the room and take the test with the opportunity to get an A grade.

Bear in mind, all the students needed to get was a B grade to pass the course, and become surgeons.

So, what did they decide? ALL but two students got up, left, accepted the B grade, and went to celebrate!

The teacher asked the only two students remaining, "I offered you a B grade without having to take the examination, so why are you still here?"

One of the students answered, "I have based my life on trying to be an A grade student and an A grade person, and I do not want to accept a B grade. So if it is alright with you, I would like to take the exam."

That was the test!

Now apply this to your life and ask the same question: A or B?

Will you choose to hold yourself to a higher standard than the outcome requires?

Will you choose A or B?

ACTION QUESTIONS

→ **What does an "A" mindset look like for you?**

THE SUNDAY SERMON

One day at a local church there was a pastor who was prepared to give the Sunday sermon and in the crowd were three older ladies who were regulars.

This particular sermon was very well received and those three ladies left talking about how beautiful and impactful it was and how they really connected with the message. Then, they went about their week living life as they normally did, before returning the following week for the next Sunday sermon.

When they arrived, they sat together in the same seats, ready with excitement in their hearts and minds to be moved by the pastor's message again. However, to their surprise, the pastor got up and preached the exact same sermon as the week before. Despite the repetition, they got up and left the church without thinking too much about what just happened.

The following week the ladies returned, and to their great astonishment, sat there as the pastor AGAIN delivered the exact same sermon as the previous two weeks. Because they were regulars, the three ladies overlooked this seemingly simple mistake on the part of the pastor and went on with their business. This went on for another couple of weeks with the pastor delivering the exact same sermon again and again until finally the three ladies decided enough was enough, and they approached the pastor to get an explanation.

In approaching the pastor, the ladies asked, "Pastor, are you aware that you have delivered the same sermon these last few weeks and do you not see anything wrong with that?"

The pastor replied, "No I don't see anything wrong with that. Now, let me ask you. Do you see anything wrong with coming here every week listening to a sermon that has the power to change your life and then not doing anything with it? I will keep preaching the same sermon until you finally apply the message to your life."

WOW!

What the pastor just explained is what I describe in the high achiever world as the SUCCESS GAP. The success gap is the distance that lies between an unsuccessful life and a successful one. And the myth is that to bridge the gap between an unsuccessful life and a successful life, all you need is KNOWLEDGE. *I will be successful when I get the next big idea, so I must consume more books, more podcasts, more videos, more articles, more sermons, more Max Moments.* The list goes on and on and on.

Now, being a continual learner is vitally important in your development. However, counter to what most people think, the success gap is not knowledge. The success gap is built on our actions and decisions. In other words, are you actually doing what you know? That is the big question. And if you are not, then why not?

Can I be honest with you? Whatever you want to succeed at in your life, you already know what to do! But here's the thing, most people don't do what they know. If they did, EVERYONE would be super achievers performing and living life at an extraordinary level!

The pastor in the story delivered knowledge that had the power to change those ladies' lives.

With reading this book, my intent is that these Max Moments provide you with some insights that can help you reach the next level in your success journey.

But my question is this...

→ When are you finally going to start taking action on what you already know?

→ When are you finally going to turn "I should do it" into "I must do it"?

→ When are you finally going to stop consuming GREAT ideas and turn them into a GREAT life?

You already have the knowledge, you just need to take the action. The great battle of life is not man against the world, it is man against the self. Win that battle today!

ACTION QUESTIONS

If you are truly honest with yourself:

→ **What knowledge do you know about creating success that you haven't used and taken action on?**

→ **Why haven't you taken action and used the knowledge even though you know it would create the success you want?**

THE FLY BAR

A French acrobat by the name of Jules Leotard performed the very first flying trapeze act at the Cirque Napoleon in Paris in 1859. His act completely wowed audiences because it involved people flying through the air at heights upwards of 40 feet and all without a safety net!

In traditional flying trapeze, there is a flier and a catcher who climb tall ladders up to a small platform. The catcher has a catch bar, and the flier has a fly bar. They both swing through the air and at the appropriate time the catcher will signal to the flier to let go. Then the flier will propel themselves through the air until the catcher, who is dangling in midair, on the other trapeze catches them!

Now here's the thing, according to many of the top trapeze performers, the greatest challenge they face when trying a new trick, because of all the potential dangers and everything that could go wrong, is what they call the "Mental Block."

Think about it for a moment. What is the hardest part of the trapeze act? Letting go. It is hard to let go of the fly bar because you are about to do something you have never done before (40 feet in the air, no less)!

Letting go of the fly bar goes against every natural instinct we have, because our natural inclination is to hold on. We want to hold on to what we have, hold on to a level of comfort, hold on to security. I am telling you right now you've got to overcome the mental block if you are going to let go of the fly bar and take your life to the next level.

When you let go of the fly bar in your life, it will mean no longer staying in your safe zone. It will mean moving out of that place of comfort and into the unknown, which is not safe. It will mean leading life with faith because you are no longer in control. But what waits on the other side of the fear and unknown when you let go of the fly bar is something truly extraordinary.

So, what fly bar do you need to let go of that is currently keeping your life at a safe level? The one that, once you let go of, will take you to the next level of success, impact, creativity, love, and abundance? And what would life look like, feel like, and be like when you finally allow yourself to let go of the fly bar?

Cirque du Soleil coach Miguel Vargas, who is a fifth generation circus performer, says that after all the training and all the repetitions are complete, all that's left is the courage to let go!

ACTION QUESTIONS

→ **What fly bar do you need to let go of that will take you to the NEXT LEVEL?**

THE GREAT ESCAPE

"I believe man was designed for
accomplishment, engineered
for success, and endowed with
the seeds of greatness."

ZIG ZIGLAR

Back in the early 1900s Harry Houdini was a master illusionist who was famous for his escape acts. Nicknamed Harry "Handcuff" Houdini he could bedazzle crowds by escaping from handcuffs, chains, ropes, and straightjackets while hanging from buildings, trapped underwater, and even while buried alive!

He was most noted for his act in which he traveled the world challenging local police to restrain him with shackles and then lock him up in their jail cells. One of the greatest escape artists of all time, he succeeded every single time except one. On this particular occasion, upon entering the jail cell he proceeded to pick the lock just like every other time. But no matter how hard Houdini tried, he couldn't unlock it. Moments turned into minutes, and minutes turned into hours, until finally he gave up in frustration. What was the problem? The officer had forgotten to lock the cell, which was unlocked the entire time. Thus, the only locked door was inside Harry Houdini's mind. The irony was that this was the only escape route he had never considered: the unlocked door!

Our outer world, what we experience, is first created in our inner world by what we believe to be true. Thus, when we create self-imposed limitations inside our minds (inner world) we will manifest them into our outer world through experiences and what we call our reality.

Fleas are another example of how easily we condition our minds to think, act, and feel in ways that shape our reality. Put a bunch of fleas into a jar, place a lid on it, and watch what happens. At first, the fleas jump to escape the jar, each time hitting up against the lid. They will continue to do this repeatedly with the thought that the same action might create a different result. Then something interesting happens. After a certain amount of time, the fleas condition their behavior to fit the environment they are in. They will still jump but only high enough so that they won't hit the lid of the jar. With the new conditioned behavior, when you take the lid off of the jar, the fleas will never escape!

We do the same thing to ourselves, don't we...

Whether through our own beliefs or the beliefs of those around us (our environment), we condition our minds to think that we only deserve and are capable of so much. As a consequence, we adjust our expectations to fit those beliefs, creating a life of mediocrity instead of abundance.

But know this for sure: YOU are capable of far more than you think. You are living a life inside your own jar and for the longest time you keep hitting your head on the lid of mediocrity. When that lid is taken off and opens you to new opportunities, the issue is that you have conditioned yourself to believe that the lid of mediocrity is still on tight, trapping you from that next level of success and fulfillment that you want and deserve in your life.

Whether you think you CAN or you think you CAN'T, either way you will be right.

If you want to make it to the next level in life, you must remove the imaginary lid of limitation and, like Harry

Houdini, unlock the door to make your great escape into the life you are truly meant to lead!

ACTION QUESTIONS

Harry Houdini's escape route was one he had never considered, the unlocked door!

→ **What is something you have never considered that will help you make your great escape?**

THE SUCCESS PENDULUM

"In any moment of decision, the best thing you can do is the right thing, the next best thing is the wrong thing, and the worst thing you can do is nothing."

THEODORE ROOSEVELT

If you were told that the key to success is to fail a lot, what would you think?

This concept can seem counterintuitive when you are advised to go out and actively experience the very opposite of what you desire. However, when we look at success and the process to achieve it as a pendulum, we can better understand its effect.

If you look at the Pendulum of Life, on one side we can find things like happiness, joy, success, victory, and love.

On the other side we will find unhappiness, pain, failure, defeat, and rejection. Now, if a pendulum does not swing at all, it will remain at rest in a position that is called equilibrium.

I believe many of us experience equilibrium in our lives when we stay locked in our comfort zone to protect ourselves from things we don't want to feel. Over time, we figure out how to operate within a very small window, and if we only allow our pendulum to swing a little into pain, failure, and rejection, then we only get to experience a fraction of joy, success, and happiness on the other side. So, by guarding ourselves from the potential of pain, we never get to experience the true fullness of life and instead we settle for a reality where we want more out of life but are not willing to do what it takes to get it.

The solution is to have the inner belief, courage, and open-mindedness to push the pendulum and swing it freely without F.E.A.R (False Evidence Appears Real). Remember...

THE PENDULUM DOES NOT SWING ONE WAY ONLY. And the more you push it, the more it swings in the other direction.

For instance, Walt Disney is a great example of swinging the pendulum. After being fired from a job because "he lacked imagination and had no good ideas," he continued to have so many more failures, including bankruptcy. Hundreds of banks rejected him when he was trying to start his business, but he kept on trying. Even worse was when he finally came up with what he thought was the great idea of a talking mouse. He was told by everyone that it would never work. But, today Mickey Mouse and the Walt Disney Company have become iconic. It was Walt Disney's desire to push the pendulum and be willing to experience major failure and rejection that swung the pendulum equally in the other direction to create the remarkable success he is known for today. As a consequence, millions of people have had the pleasure of sharing in the fun, happiness, and enjoyment that his vision has given the world through movies, lovable characters, and theme parks! As he said, "If you can dream it, you can do it. Remember that this whole thing started with a dream and a mouse."

So, as the person in charge of your Pendulum of Life you control how high and how far you wish to swing the pendulum. Will it be scary to push the pendulum outside of the comfort zone that you set for yourself? Absolutely. Will you experience more failure, rejection, pain, and defeat as a result? Absolutely. Will it create the potential for the pendulum to swing back in the other direction toward something far greater that you can't even imagine yet? Absolutely.

So do the right thing and push the pendulum a little higher today...

ACTION QUESTIONS

→ **What area of your life do you need to push the pendulum of failure to experience more success?**

WHO NEEDS SHOES AND SOCKS

Jim Thorpe was an athlete from Oklahoma who became an Olympic gold medalist that taught us about the importance of a strong mindset and never giving up.

There is a famous picture of Jim Thorpe competing at the 1912 Olympics in Stockholm, Sweden. The picture shows him wearing his USA uniform along with two completely different shoes and two completely different socks. This was not a fashion statement, but a desperate attempt to improvise after his shoes were stolen on the morning of his track and field competition at the Olympics!

According to Bob Wheeler, founder of the Jim Thorpe foundation and author of the biography *Jim Thorpe: The*

World's Greatest Athlete, on the morning of his race Jim had a teammate reportedly lend him one of his shoes and Thorpe found another shoe in a garbage can just so he could compete. What's even more incredible is that he had to wear extra socks to make them fit since one of the shoes was too big. Despite all of that, Jim Thorpe went on to win two gold medals that day in the high jump and the 110-meter hurdles. Amazing!

Despite what most people think, our successes and what we can and will achieve in life never comes down to resources. Jim Thorpe did not win gold that day because he had better resources than the other participants. He did not have the latest pair of Nikes or groundbreaking technology to give him the upper hand. He didn't even have his own personal equipment, but what he had was an inner fire and hunger to succeed.

When it comes to what you want in your life, it is never going to be a matter of the resources you have. Instead, it is always going to be a matter of your resourcefulness in finding what you need, so that you can get what you want. I know many people, teams, and organizations that have everything in terms of resources, and yet they don't use it to create an equal amount of success and contribution in this world. Why? Because resources are never the problem. If they were, then Jim Thorpe should not have won two gold medals that day at the Olympics. It will always be a matter of how resourceful you are willing to be.

What Jim Thorpe's story can teach us is when you are hungry enough, determined enough, willing enough, curious enough, flexible enough, and creative enough, then you can and will find a way to make your dreams become a reality.

ACTION QUESTIONS

→ **Where are you holding back because you think you don't have the right resources, but really you aren't hungry enough?**

SLOW DOWN TO SPEED UP

The idea of training slower to race faster is counterintuitive. How can a runner possibly be capable of running at their very best when they need it most, if they do not frequently train at that pace? The typical mindset has always been "more is better," right?

Now this concept of "more is better" doesn't just apply to running, but to any high performer who has visions of trying to hit the next level. You see many high performers fall into a trap called the "Gray Zone." In running terms, it is the trap of training in a zone where you aren't going easy enough to get the benefits of a nice easy workout and you aren't going hard enough to get the benefits of a race pace workout. The problem is that continual work in this gray zone does not allow for enough recovery. It's like trying to perform in a state of constant fatigue.

If we are honest with ourselves, isn't that how many of us operate in life? We try to do everything and be everything. We always want to do more. So, like the runner, our expectation is that if we just run faster and faster trying to cram more and more into our daily schedule that it will benefit us. But by running faster, all we are really doing is constantly operating in the gray zone and in a state of fatigue. We are ingraining poor habits that ultimately inhibit our progression and development toward reaching that next level. Thus, we settle for mediocre results instead of extraordinary results.

So counter to what most people do, the actual answer for many top performers is to SLOW DOWN!

We have to slow down to speed up. Yes, that is right, we have to slow down to speed up!

By slowing down, what it actually does is give us time and space to breathe and evaluate our life differently. That way we can show back up to the most important parts of our life in a more powerful way, be at the top of our game, and gain the desired results.

This is the difference between good and great!

You can spend your whole life in the gray zone and just be good. Some people might be ok with that. But for the people who choose to be great and want something more, it starts by slowing down.

I will give you an example.

Thomas Edison was a genius who invented many things, including the phonograph, the motion picture camera, and, what he is most known for, the electric lightbulb. What you may not know is that he was a terrible fisherman.

He used to spend an hour every day fishing, but never caught any fish. You might be wondering how that is possible. How can someone spend so much time fishing and never catch anything?

Well, someone once asked him that exact question and here was his response: "I never caught any fish because I never used any bait!"

And when asked why he would fish without bait, he said, "Because when you fish without bait, people don't bother you, and neither do the fish. So it provides me with my best time to think!"

Amazing, right?

If you want to be a top performer, set aside some time for yourself to think, reflect, and be creative. Make it a priority. Because if you want to race faster, start by going slower!

ACTION QUESTIONS

→ **What are three ways you can slow down and take time for yourself?**

→ **How will slowing down help you speed up?**

10 SECONDS OF COURAGE

Have you ever jumped out of a plane? I have, and it was one of the scariest and most exhilarating experiences I have ever had.

Whenever you jump out of an airplane, you need a parachute, and it will only work when it is opened. Obvious, I know, but true. What is not as obvious is how the same principle works for our mindset...

Just as a parachute only works when it is open, our mind works best when it is open. Open-mindedness is an amazing quality to have because it opens us up to new possibilities. But when we live with a closed mindset, we are closing doors to opportunities before they have even opened, opportunities that have the power to change the course of our lives forever.

And one thing that gets in the way of us going after a new possibility is fear. You see, fear is an illusion that we create in our minds and that illusion can only exist in the absence of reality. Once we experience the reality of a situation, then the illusion we create in our mind goes away. When you think about when we feel fear, it mostly comes from the anticipation of the experience and what we imagine is about to happen, not from the experience itself.

I know this for a fact because I felt this when I jumped out of that plane at 10,000ft!

In fact, there was a study conducted by Seymour Epstein at the University of Massachusetts Amherst where novice jumpers (like myself) were fitted with heart rate monitors that measured their pulses as the plane climbed towards its release point, which for me was 10,000ft.

After compiling all the data, what he found was that the jumpers' heart rates got faster and faster as the plane got higher and higher, and the jumpers' heart rates were highest right before they jumped out of the plane. But here is the crazy part: once they jumped out of the plane, their heart rates declined dramatically.

So what this study showed was that the most stressful part of the entire experience was not the jump but rather the illusion that was created in their mind about what they thought would happen. Once they jumped out of the plane and began free-falling, the reality of the event took over and guess what happened: the fear vanished!

This is a great reminder of what we are missing out on in life if we let our fear close the door on possibility. Why? Because we make things out in our minds to be more than they are! So, what is the antidote to that wall of fear and the illusion we create in our minds? 10 seconds of courage! All it takes is 10 seconds of courage to get you past the anticipation and just go for it!

I can still remember that day vividly. I stood at the door of the plane with my toes on the edge, looking out at the world from a perspective I had never experienced before. My heart was pumping, I was scared, and I had done all the things that the study shared. I had created such a high level of fear in my mind because of the anticipation of the moment that I almost didn't jump. What took over in that moment was 10 seconds of insane courage! I let go, and I went for it. On the other side of those 10 seconds was the reality, I got to experience the adrenaline of life at a level I never had before.

Imagine if you applied this principle. Imagine the possibility. Imagine what 10 seconds of courage could do to help you create new breakthroughs and experience life at the level I know you want to get to!

ACTION QUESTIONS

Closed Mindset:

→ **What is an event that you never got to experience because your mind made it out to be more than it was (the fear you had in anticipation of the event)?**

Open Mindset:

→ **What is an event that you got to experience because you used 10 seconds of courage to get past the anticipation and just go for it?**

MAX MOMENTS ON HABITS

THE POWER OF PARETO

"In any series of elements to be controlled, a selected small fraction, in terms of numbers of elements, always accounts for a large fraction in terms of effect."

VILFREDO PARETO

Are you familiar with the Pareto Principle? The Pareto Principle is something that shows up a lot in our daily lives, we may not even be aware of its impact. This principle, more commonly known as the 80/20 rule, states that in many cases, about 80% of the effects come from 20% of the causes.

This observation is named after an economist in the early 1900s named Vilfredo Pareto, who found that about 20% of the population in Italy (where he was living) owned

80% of the land. He also discovered about 20% of the peapods in his garden were producing 80% of the peas. This led him to the rationale that many things in life are not distributed evenly. Now the numbers will not always be exactly 80/20, but it does prove that a few things account for a majority of the results.

Here are just a few of the areas where the Pareto Principle can show up:

- ➜ 80% of results are created by 20% of the output.

- ➜ 80% of problems are attributed to 20% of the causes.

- ➜ 80% of company profits come from 20% of the clients.

- ➜ 80% of business complaints come from 20% of the customers.

- ➜ 80% of traffic occurs during 20% of the day.

- ➜ 80% of the time you wear 20% of your wardrobe.

- ➜ 80% of team issues come from 20% of team members.

- ➜ 80% of training results come from 20% of your habits.

- ➜ 80% of championships are won by 20% of the teams.

We can apply it to our lives by understanding that focusing on the vital few things (the 20%) in particular areas of our life can create the massive results that we desire (the 80%). The 80/20 rule shows us that a few habits and choices will account for the majority of our success and happiness. Therefore, the seemingly small inconsequential choices we decide to make consistently each day have a huge impact on the life we lead and how it will ultimately shape our destiny.

Mastering the 80/20 lifestyle is about narrowing our focus toward what we can control and committing to doing the little, daily things that will make a big difference over time.

It is about deciding to make the smallest shifts to create the biggest impact.

It is about being process oriented rather than results driven.

It is about having big goals and dreams whilst understanding the way to achieve them is through discipline in the smallest details.

It is about knowing the highest form of fulfillment can come in the littlest act of kindness and gratitude.

It is knowing that the big events will show up in our life once we first seek to discover their small causes.

So let me ask you this...

→ What 20% of daily habits can you commit to that will add 80% value to your life?

→ What 20% shift in focus could you have that will make you feel 80% happier?

→ What 20% of problems must you let go of to lift 80% of your burden and worry?

→ What 20% of barriers are holding you back from making an 80% breakthrough?

Finally...

WHAT 20% OF DECISIONS WILL YOU MAKE TODAY THAT WILL HAVE AN 80% IMPACT ON YOUR LIFE?

ACTION QUESTIONS

→ **What is one small choice (20%) you can make that will have a big impact (80%) on your life?**

DO YOU SPEND TIME VS. INVEST TIME

Do you currently SPEND time or INVEST time?

To some, this may sound like the same thing, but as we will discover, there is a big difference between the two, because which word you choose will directly affect the direction your life is heading. How you use your time tells yourself and everyone around you what you value. Looking at your schedule and seeing what you are committed to will also show exactly who you are and, more importantly, who you are becoming.

SPEND

To spend means to use something up or exhaust it. When we spend time, we are typically seeking an activity to help us pass the time or change our state and we only gain short-term pleasure without long-term benefit.

INVEST

To invest means to expend resources, but with the expectation of gaining a return on that investment. When we invest time, we are seeking and engaging in activities which will bring about more meaningful rewards and longer term results.

For instance:

- ➤ Are you spending time complaining about your problems or investing time in finding a solution?

- ➤ Are you spending time working at a job that just pays the bills or investing time in a profession that fulfills your life's purpose?

- ➤ Are you spending time watching reruns of your favorite TV shows or investing time in reading books that will expand your knowledge?

- ➤ Are you spending time with people who settle for less than they can be or investing time in a network of people that want more and challenge you to grow?

➔ Are you spending time improving yourself
   as an athlete only at scheduled practice or
   investing time by yourself to become the very
   best you can be?

➔ Are you spending time in class at the back of
   the room just because you have to be there
   or investing time by sitting at the front and
   engaging in the lecture because you have an
   opportunity to learn and obtain an education
   others can only dream of?

➔ Are you spending time paralyzed by emotions
   of fear, worry, and frustration or investing
   time in empowering emotions of faith, love
   and gratitude?

What we focus on, we get more of, and what we give our
attention to is what we will attract. Thus, we must INVEST
our time in activities that align with our goals, dreams,
aspirations and vision in order to achieve what we desire.

John Wooden, considered one of the greatest basketball
coaches of all time by winning 10 national championships (seven in a row), is a wonderful example of how the
successful INVEST their time. After a grueling season,
most coaches & players take a break, but Coach Wooden
developed a different habit. After the basketball season

ended, instead of celebrating the championship, he would immediately turn his attention to the next season and how he could get better. He would simply choose one basketball or coaching technique to improve and then immerse himself for two to three weeks in researching everything he could about that topic. This investment each year was how he was able to continue growing as a coach, lead a successful college program, and overcome complacency, which is often synonymous with winning and success.

Having lived in the world of high performance for the last 20 plus years, one of the most common things I hear is, "I don't have enough time." So, let's do a quick equation to show how easy investing our time can be: Say you really wanted to learn a new skill. If you commit 20 minutes of your daily schedule, 5 times a week to investing in the activity, over the course of one year you will have invested 86 extra hours in that activity!

Could you find 20 minutes in your current schedule to invest in something that is important to you? Of course you could, but here is what people do instead...

Some will choose to watch TV for an extra 20 minutes, rather than read the book.

Some will choose to scroll through social media for 20 minutes, rather than work out.

Some will choose to hit the snooze button and sleep in rather than having a productive morning.

The choice is yours, but ultimately, we all get what we must have. Nobody is ever too busy. It's just a matter of priorities!

What if I could give you an extra two weeks a year that you could do anything with? Would you like that? Everyone would! Well, how do you get an extra two weeks a year? Don't waste 20 minutes! The math is pretty simple. Based on the average work week of 40 hours, 20 wasted minutes each day is the equivalent to two 40-hour workweeks at the end of the year. Think what you could do with two weeks a year!

Make the choice to stop SPENDING time on things that will only lead you to fall short of your potential. Instead, INVEST in the opportunities and activities that will help you live into your greatest potential.

You were born to be extraordinary, so INVEST in that!

ACTION QUESTIONS

- ➜ What is a skill or area you want to get better at?
- ➜ How would improving in that area help you?
- ➜ Commit to scheduling 20 mins each day to work on it!

A LIFE WITH KAIZEN

"Whoever wants to reach a distant goal must take small steps."

HELMUT SCHMIDT

Kaizen is the Japanese word for continual improvement or changing for the better. It most commonly refers to a long-term approach to seeking small, incremental changes that will create larger, more impactful results over time. Many businesses have used the concept of Kaizen as a way to improve functionality and efficiency within their teams, their processes, and their products. However, the Kaizen principles used in business can also apply to self-improvement and personal success.

Many people want instant success and therefore look for the quickest way to obtain it. This mindset causes us to think that the right thing to do is make radical changes in the shortest amount of time possible. This approach is drastic, unsustainable, and while it may produce results in the short term, it does not set us up for long-term success. Instead, we need to operate under Kaizen principles, which focus on small improvements that are manageable and sustainable, making it easier to follow through more consistently, creating the continual improvement needed for success.

An example of this is the amazing story of David Brailsford and the Team Sky cycling team. In 2010, David took over as the general manager of the Team Sky cycling team with the seemingly impossible task of becoming the first ever British cycling team to win the Tour De France. He quickly adopted the principles of Kaizen and looked for every way in which he could improve the process and efficiency of the team.

He explained it as "the 1 percent margin for improvement in everything we do." If he could improve every area related to cycling by just 1 percent, then those small gains would add up to a significant improvement. They began by finding 1 percent improvements in their training program, diet and nutrition, the bike seat, the weight of the tires, the shape of the helmets and the fabric the cyclists wore. They went even deeper to search for the seemingly insignificant 1 percent improvements such as what bed and pillow offered the best sleep, as well as the best hygiene practices to avoid unnecessary illness and the best massage gels.

What was the result of these 1 percent improvements as they all added up? In just two years, Team Sky rider Bradley Wiggins became the first British cyclist to win the Tour De France in 2012! Since then, they have continued their success winning the Tour De France in 2013, 2015, 2016, 2017, 2018 and 2019!

As Jim Rohn says, "Success is a few simple disciplines, practiced every day; while failure is simply a few errors in judgment repeated every day."

Improving by just 1 percent often isn't noticeable, but with a Kaizen mindset, you come to understand that even a 1 percent improvement can be the difference. Each small step of progress, every day, added up over time, has the power to change your life for the better. The Kaizen philosophy knows that no moment, action, or choice, no matter how big or small, is insignificant.

When you begin living a life of Kaizen, you will understand this powerful saying from Rory Vaden: "Success

is never owned; it is only rented, and the rent is
due every day."

ACTION QUESTIONS

→ **What 1 percent improvement can you make
today that has the potential to change your life?**

DON'T BREAK THE CHAIN

This little productivity hack will help you create winning habits in life. It comes from the successful stand-up comedian and star of the television sitcom *Seinfeld*, which is widely regarded as one of the greatest and most influential sitcoms of all time. And of course I am talking about the comic Jerry Seinfeld!

Jerry, like many extraordinarily successful people, frequently gets asked what has been the key to his rise in fame, fortune, and success. In his answers, he always points back to a time when he was just starting out working the stage at open mic nights doing stand-up comedy and just trying to make a name for himself.

To be a brilliant comedian, he said, you have to have great content and funny jokes. When he first started out, he would randomly write down ideas and things when they came to him without rhyme or reason. But then he made one small shift that ultimately made an extraordinary difference in the results he created in his career, and it was this. . . .

He made a COMMITMENT to write one joke a day. Just one. Seems simple, I know. He would not write an entire act or routine, just one funny line. Then he would do it the next day, and the day after that and the day after that, until he was consistently writing funny content all the time.

But this is the part that really made the difference: To make sure he stayed consistent and created the habit of writing one joke every day, he got a big calendar and put it up on the wall in his apartment. For every day that he wrote a joke or funny line, he would put a big red X on the calendar for that day. Through his consistency, before long he had a long chain of big red X's that he could visually see every time he looked at the calendar on the wall. Soon that calendar became a visual representation of the momentum he had created, the path he was on, and the consistent work he had put in. So much so that writing material was no longer about having to create jokes, it became about putting another red X on the calendar and not leaving a single day blank.

Jerry Seinfeld shared this story with a young comic who was curious to know about his key to success, and the advice Jerry gave him was simply this: DON'T BREAK THE CHAIN!

It sounds so easy, and I know what you are thinking. Something so simple can't possibly be the key to success, can it? But what is easy to do is also easy not to do. That's why not everyone will do it, and that's what makes it so genius.

As easy as it sounds to not break the chain, when life happens and gets in the way (and you know the stuff I am talking about), we must make decisions. It is in these moments of decision that we find out how important it is to us whether or not to break the chain.

This concept of not breaking the chain can apply to literally anything:

- ➔ It can apply to writing, music, art, or anything creative

- ➔ It can apply to reading for personal development

- ➔ It can apply to working out consistently to get fit or train for a big event

- ➔ It can apply to eating better to improve your health and vitality

➔ It can apply to doing extra training to improve a certain skill

➔ It can apply to doing something nice for someone to show your appreciation

Apply it to whatever you want to get better at. Apply it to whatever you want to create a new level of success in. Just apply it and commit to doing it every day, NO EXCEPTIONS. Even if you can't commit two hours to your chosen endeavor, fifteen minutes is better than not at all. Your goal should not be perfection; your goal should be to not break the chain.

Personally, I used to think that if I did not have one entire hour to work out, then it was not worth it and I would not work out. Some days I would get a great workout in and other days I wouldn't do anything. Now I realize that twenty minutes is better than not working out at all. It might not be my ideal workout, but something is better than nothing. and in the process, I am teaching myself to not break the chain.

If you are one of the few who stays consistent and does not break the chain, working on building success in your life day after day, week after week, and year after year, then the rewards will be beyond anything you can imagine!

This is now my simple formula for success:

Today + Today + Today + Today + Today +
Today + Today + Today = Your Destiny

Do it today. Grab a calendar, start tallying up those X's, and don't break the chain!

ACTION QUESTIONS

→ **How long do you think you can do something important to improve your life without breaking the chain?**

WHICH DIRECTION DO YOU SWIM

Our lives and the results we create are determined by the choices we make each and every day. So, the big question to ask is: how do we know which are the right choices to make?

Are you ready for this? When faced with a difficult choice, select the hardest one. It is that simple! Normally what you DON'T want to do is the very thing you SHOULD do. Yet many people often select the path of LEAST resistance that is comfortable. Instead we need to be seeking the path of MOST resistance that is uncomfortable. To get the results we want in life, we need to stop doing the things we feel like doing and start doing the less glamorous, uncomfortable things that will stretch and grow us.

I liken this decision-making process to swimming in a river. Swimming downstream with the current is what most people do every day of their lives. Choosing to swim downstream is easy and comfortable, with little to no resistance. As creatures of habit, we mindlessly get swept along the river of life and, if we are not careful, will end up in a place we did not consciously choose.

Examples of downstream choices:

- ➔ Only doing what is expected and nothing more.

- ➔ Giving into peer pressure and following the crowd.

- ➔ Staying inside your comfort zone.

But for those who desire something greater from life, there is another far less traveled option we can take: swim in the other direction! Swimming upstream against life's current will undoubtedly come with significant resistance, is going to be very difficult, and will definitely be uncomfortable, which is why so few people will choose to do it. But swimming upstream can also take you to places others only dream of.

Examples of upstream choices:

→ Being willing to go the extra mile.

→ Saying no when others want you to say yes.

→ Feeling fearful and taking action, anyway.

If you want to create a different result, then make a different choice. Stop settling for the path of least resistance and start pursuing the path of most resistance. Start doing difficult things and whatever you try to avoid at all costs. Because those are exactly the things that will take you to the next level. Let's be honest, if you were to dedicate yourself to ONLY doing the things you DON'T want to do all day long, the results would blow you away! But are you also willing to make the sacrifices it takes?

For instance, take something in your life right now that you would like to change. Now, identify the daily choices you are currently making in that area and start doing the complete opposite. It really is that simple!

Start being comfortable being uncomfortable...

This is a life-changing decision. Which way are you going to swim in the river of life: UPSTREAM or DOWNSTREAM?

The choice is yours...

ACTION QUESTIONS

→ **What is an area of your life that you want to improve?**

→ **What daily choices are you currently making in that area?**

→ **What upstream choices must you make that will help you improve in that area?**

THE GUARANTEED SUCCESS FORMULA

JP Morgan was a successful banker and philanthropist who was once offered a sealed envelope containing advice on what was described as the "Guaranteed Success Formula."

He agreed that if he liked the advice written inside, he would pay the asking price of $25,000 for its contents (which was a lot of money back then)!

JP Morgan took the envelope, carefully opened it, and pulled out a single piece of paper. He read the advice, nodded, and then wrote a check for $25,000 on the spot.

So, what was the "Guaranteed Success Formula"?

There were only 2 things written on the sheet of paper:

1. Every morning, write a list of the most important things that need to be done that day.

2. Do them.

Are you surprised? It sounds too obvious, right?

Of course, it's common sense, but just because it is common sense does not make it common practice. That is what separates the good from the great. It's the great ones that align what they think, what they say, and what they do. They have great habits and make smart, consistent choices each day. Ultimately, they do what they say they are going to do and remain true to their word. Most importantly, they are loyally committed to doing the thing they said they were going to do long after the "right" mood has left.

When you live with integrity and make your word your world, amazing things can happen for you in your life. Make your word a commitment and say I AM GOING TO MAKE THIS HAPPEN! When you do, you will be one of the few who do versus the many who don't.

ACTION QUESTIONS

➔ What are the most important things you need to get done today that will move you in the direction of the success you desire?

➔ Once you write the list. DO THEM!

INSIDE OUT

Once, there was a gentleman who was visiting a temple under construction. While on the premises, he saw a sculptor who was making a statue of God. Just a few feet away, he saw another identical statue of God laying on the ground. Surprised, he asked the sculptor, "Do you need two statues of the same figure?"

"No," said the sculptor, "we only need one, but the first one got damaged."

The gentleman examined the sculpture and saw no apparent damage, so he asked the sculptor, "Where is the damage?"

"Well, there is a scratch on the nose of the figure," said the sculptor.

"Huh, well it's barely visible, where are you going to place the statue?"

"It is going to be placed on top of that 20 foot pillar," said the sculptor.

The gentleman replied, "Really, but when that statue is 20 feet away from the eyes of the observer, who is going to know that there is a scratch on the nose?"

The sculptor looked at the gentleman, smiled, and said, "I will know, and God will also!"

High achievers should desire to excel and achieve success whether anyone will see it or not. Because it is not for somebody else to notice, but for our own satisfaction. Why?

Excellence is a drive that comes from the inside out, not the outside in.

Similarly, a great carpenter isn't going to use lousy wood for the back of a cabinet, even though nobody's going to see it. Now an average carpenter might try to cut corners, but not a great one. Why?

Excellence is a drive that comes from the inside out, not the outside in.

You don't climb a mountain with the intention of reaching the peak and having the world see you. You climb a mountain with the intention of reaching the peak so you can see the world. Why?

Excellence is a drive that comes from the inside out, not the outside in.

And the same is true in your life. Your desire to achieve a high level of excellence should not be affected by whether anyone else will see it. Do it because it is the right thing to do. Do it because of the impact it will have. Do it because when you let your light shine from the inside out, extraordinary things can and will happen in your life!

ACTION QUESTIONS

→ **What ways do you "do the right thing" when no one else is watching, which impact your success?**

→ **What ways do you "do the wrong thing" when no one else is watching, which impacts your success?**

CRAZY MATH THAT WILL CHANGE YOUR LIFE

I live my life seeking ways to help people understand the smallest shifts that can create extraordinary results in their life. Once implemented, these small shifts have the power to change our lives, and the mathematical equivalent of these changes is known as exponential growth.

To help you understand the idea of exponential growth, let's use math to see how you can reach the moon by folding a single piece of paper. You heard that right, folding a single piece of paper can get you to the moon!

Let's assume that you have a single piece of paper that is the standard 0.1 mm thick. Let's also assume that the size of the paper is big enough that you can fold it over and over as many times as you wish. Now let me ask you, how many times would you have to fold the piece of paper for it to be thick enough to reach the moon?

Think about it for a moment before you continue reading...

If we fold the paper once, it would be 0.2mm thick. If we fold it a second time, it would be 0.4mm thick and if we fold it for a third time, it would be 0.8mm thick. Get it so far. So if the number doubles every time, what is the number that gets us to the moon?

That number is 42 times! If you need to check the math before you believe me, you can, but the number is 42. If you were like me when I first tried to work it out, I thought it would be thousands and thousands.

So how do we get from a thickness of 0.1mm to a thickness of 239,000 miles in 42 folds? The power of exponential growth is how. This is crazy math that will change your life!

The reason for sharing this crazy math is simply to reinforce that the little things in life can make the biggest difference. If you want to make a significant change in your life, don't underestimate the power of the little things. A single piece of paper folded enough times can get you to the moon, and the same is true in your life. A single, small positive change repeated consistently over time can get you where you want to go. But you cannot give up. Let the crazy math work for you.

One last thing to show you the power of the little things. One piece of paper folded 42 times can get you to the moon. Well, if you fold it just one more time, that same piece of paper will get you to the moon AND all the way back to earth, which is a round trip close to half a million miles!

ACTION QUESTIONS

➤ **Where in your life have you previously given up on something and not allowed the crazy math to take effect and create extraordinary results?**

➤ **Where in your life can you make a small positive change that, if you allow the crazy math to take effect, can create extraordinary results?**

MAX MOMENTS ON RESILIENCE

PUT THE GLASS DOWN

This is a simple story about a glass of water. There was a psychology professor who walked around a room one day while teaching stress management to her students. As she was lecturing, she was holding a glass of water, and everyone expected they'd be asked the normal question: is the glass half empty or half full? Which would then trigger a debate about how your perception of the glass is dependent upon the attitude of the person looking at it.

The pessimists in the room would say it was half empty.

The optimists would say it was half full.

Instead, the teacher asked this question:

"How heavy is this glass of water?"

Answers blurted out ranged from 8 oz. all the way to 20 oz.

The teacher's reply was a lesson in resilience and how to overcome adversity. She said: "The absolute weight of the glass doesn't matter. It depends on how long you hold it. If you hold the glass for a minute, it's not a problem. If you hold the glass for an hour, you will have an ache in your arm. If you hold the glass for a day, your arm will feel numb and paralyzed. In each case, the weight of the glass doesn't change, but the longer you hold it, the heavier it becomes."

She continued, "the stresses and worries found in life are like that glass of water. Think about them for a little while and nothing happens. Think about them a bit longer and they begin to hurt. And if you think about them all day long, you will feel paralyzed and incapable of doing anything."

So the message that day was plain and simple. Put the glass down!

In reality, many people struggle with being able to let go of past mistakes and failures. Holding onto the glass for longer than needed creates a stacking of negative emotions, causing added pressure and an inability to take consistent and intentional action towards their desired result.

To help you "put the glass down" you need to focus on the three Ps: Present, Positive, and Process.

- → Focus on the PRESENT: Put down your glass that is full of past failures and future fears. Because once you put that glass down, you can get laser focused and invest your time and energy into the one block of time you have total control over, which is the PRESENT moment.

- → Focus on the POSITIVE: Put down your glass that is full of negative thoughts about all the things that are holding you back and all that you are trying to avoid in your life. Because once you put that glass down, you can focus on all the POSITIVE things that you want to attract and create in your life.

- → Focus on the PROCESS: Put down your glass that is full of self-imposed destinations and outcomes you believe you must achieve in order to feel significant and successful. Because once you put that glass down, you can focus on what is most important, the journey, and commit fully

to the PROCESS of daily growth to reach your
maximum potential.

If you want to succeed in life, remember that your past
does not equal your future. Instead, make a life altering
decision and decide to put down the glass that has been
holding you back from the next level you desire!

ACTION QUESTIONS

→ **What glass are you still holding onto that you
need to put down?**

THE PROBLEM WITH PROBLEMS

What is a major problem in your life right now?

What is a massive cause of concern or stress for you right now?

What is something that you just can't seem to get past?

Take all of that and then let me add this caveat...

What if that problem is actually providing you with your greatest opportunity?

Sounds crazy, I know. But the problem with problems is that most people don't view them correctly. We think that successful people shouldn't have problems or when we do have problems, all they do is prevent us from reaching the level of success we desire.

Looking back, what past problems have you allowed to stop you from creating your future successes?

When I look at success and how to achieve it, I think of what author Thomas Fuller said:

> "It is always darkest just before the
> day dawneth."

In other words, things often seem to be at their worst right before they get better. Often a setback is actually a setup to get us exactly where we are destined to be. Often the opportunity we need to get where we want to go is disguised as impossible obstacles and problems.

That is why I love working with high-achievers to help shift this perspective and show them what's possible in their life, even if they can't see it for themselves yet. That process is the practice of reframing. Reframing is about shifting focus, and if you want to take advantage of every opportunity, then you have to learn to shift your focus and start seeing your problems in a different way.

In the world of high performance, everyone is looking for the advantage, everyone is looking for the edge, everyone is looking for the little things that can ultimately make the biggest difference. For the extraordinary among us, reframing to view setbacks as opportunities, problems as blessings, and failures as gifts, is what sets them apart from everyone else.

Where others see problems, high achievers see opportunities...

You might be reading this thinking that this is way easier said than done. You might be thinking that I don't understand how bad your problems are and what you are going through. I do understand because there is nothing more difficult than trying to stay positive when nothing seems to be going your way. But I also know this: one of the key differences I have found in super achievers creating abundant success is their capacity to see their problems as opportunities. When things are darkest, they know the dawn is near. They make it less about changing their circumstances and more about changing their perspective.

If you are truly honest with yourself right now, maybe your biggest problem is not your biggest problem. Maybe your biggest problem is your perspective of the problems you currently have. Maybe you should stop wanting to avoid the difficult problems, and start asking what you are going to gain and learn from these difficult problems.

If you change your perspective, you will also change your reality. If you change your reality, you will change your life. In doing so, you will get to a place where you become as grateful for the problems as you are for the achievements. When you do that, you will enter into a realm of thinking that is reserved for a select few who know exactly how to answer this question:

What if the future you really want is hiding behind your biggest problem?

ACTION QUESTIONS

→ **What is one of your biggest problems?**

→ **With a change in perspective, how could this problem be an opportunity?**

THE ART OF KINTSUGI

There is this fascinating concept called Kintsugi, the Japanese art of putting broken pottery pieces back together. This beautiful art form can teach us a lot about how to view the adversity in our life.

Let me start by asking, what do you think most people do when they break a cup, a plate, or a bowl? They probably do one of two things:

1. Throw it away because they deem it unusable.

2. Try to glue the pieces back together perfectly and hide where it's broken.

However, with the art of Kintsugi, it is different. This tradition is built on the idea of actually embracing flaws and embracing imperfections to create an even stronger and more beautiful piece of art. To create Kintsugi art, when a piece of pottery breaks, every break is considered unique. Instead of repairing an item like new, the artist actually highlights the "scars" by using gold to paint the cracks as a part of the design when putting the pieces back together.

So how does this apply to someone like you who wants to live life at an extraordinary level?

Well, first I think we all need to admit that in some way we are broken. We want to make it look like we have it all together and we are in control, when in reality under the surface that may not be the case. The truth is, we all have our flaws, chips, cracks, and things we are working on and working through and that's ok because it is part of the process and part of our journey to get where we ultimately want to go.

The art of Kintsugi is revealing a way to reframe our mindset, and show us that we are actually better with our golden cracks. Whatever adversity you are dealing with, a mindset of Kintsugi can be a way to reframe hardships to remind you that you are not a victim of your circumstance, and that all you are going through is actually meant to help you and not hurt you. It is showing up in your life to make you better and not worse, to make you stronger and not weaker, and to propel you toward what you want and not further away.

I know it can seem counterintuitive to think we are meant to celebrate all the bad things that happen to us. But if you really stop and pause for a second, it becomes possible in this moment of awareness to see that the idea of Kintsugi can actually open you up to new possibilities and unlock the next level that may have been eluding you.

The art of Kintsugi is showing us that you can create an even more beautiful and extraordinary level of life when you embrace the flaws and imperfections and turn them into golden cracks that help you become WHO you are meant to be. So that you can go out into this world and DO what you are meant to do!

ACTION QUESTIONS

→ **What adversity have you experienced that you consider a flaw, crack, or imperfection?**

→ **Using a Kintsugi mindset to reframe, how can you look at this adversity in a way to see that it has helped you instead of hurt you?**

→ **What would embracing imperfections in your life and turning them into "Golden Cracks" do for you?**

THE PEBBLE IN YOUR SHOE

During one of my workouts, I was running on the treadmill as usual. I was in the zone, listening to my music, pounding away, as I knocked out mile after mile. But it was during this particular run that I was faced with a feeling I had not really felt before, and it was one that I could not shake. You see, every step I took, I could feel a small pebble that had found its way into my shoe and was rubbing against my foot as I took each step. Have you had that happen to you before?

It's annoying, right? But I felt it would be inconvenient to stop the treadmill so I tried to power through and continue on. But as I did so, my focus began to slowly drift away from the goal of completing the workout to this increasingly annoying feeling in my shoe. It became this battle of whether to stop and get off the treadmill or keep going. I tried and tried until finally I could not take it anymore and jumped off the treadmill to take my shoe off and get that pebble out of there!

As silly as this was, it really got me thinking about what many of us go through as we run our own race of life each day. As we pursue our goals, dreams, and desires, we are faced with "pebbles in our shoes." Not actual pebbles like the one I had in my shoe, but more so the nagging thoughts and emotions (baggage) we carry with us that weigh us down on our journey. Not each little pebble in our life is intrusive or detectable, yet it is still present daily and will ultimately become the very thing holding us back from living and experiencing the life we want.

Although a pebble in your shoe is an irritating and uncomfortable feeling, it is bearable, and because it is bearable, we don't do anything about it and learn to live with it. We learn to live with these pebbles so much that it may get to the point where it creates something called learned helplessness. This is when a person suffers from a sense of powerlessness because they feel they can't do anything to change their current situation and so they just learn to live with whatever hand they have been dealt. Have you felt this way before?

These pebbles will pop up and provide challenges in multiple areas of life: personal, professional, relational, and teams. Examples of pebbles that show up in life can be: a fear pebble, an anger pebble, a worry pebble, a frustration pebble, a jealousy pebble, a guilt pebble, a rejection pebble, and the list goes on...

It would better serve us to focus on what we can control and the amazing opportunities we have been blessed with each and every day. Because what's wrong in our life is always available, but so is what's right.

My encouragement for you is to reach into your shoes (your mind) and throw out all the pebbles that have been holding you back. Take your pebbles of fear, anger, and frustration and trade them for a strong foundation built on faith, love, and possibility.

ACTION QUESTIONS

→ **What are some small pebbles that you have learned to live with?**

→ **What does a resilient mindset look like for you?**

SHIPWRECKED

There was once a shipwreck and the lone survivor found themselves washed up on a small, deserted island. Being all alone day after day, he prayed to God to rescue him, and every day he scanned the horizon for help, but no help ever came. The days turned into weeks and still his prayers were not answered. Physically and mentally exhausted, he eventually managed to build a little hut out of driftwood and palm leaves to protect himself from the elements.

One day, after scavenging for food and water, he arrived back to find his little hut in flames with the smoke billowing into the sky above. In that moment, he realized the very worst had happened. He lost everything, including his hope. He was angry, grief-stricken, crying, and shouting, "God, how could you do this to me?"

Early the next morning, he was awakened by the sound of a ship that was approaching the island. It had come to rescue him! Once aboard the ship, he asked his rescuers, "This is a miracle. How did you know I was here?"

They replied, "We saw your smoke signal!"

Isn't it easy for us to get discouraged when things go wrong in our lives or when life doesn't go as we planned? It is easy for us to lose hope in the midst of our pain and suffering. Now what we can do when we feel ship-wrecked in our life and our hut is burning to the ground is to provide a reframe.

Reframing is changing what something means by seeing it through a different frame of reference. To do that means finding an empowering meaning, no matter what happens in your life. Or put another way, finding a way to appreciate and be grateful for EVERYTHING that happens in your life, EVEN in the midst of the pain and suffering.

There is also something called a "context reframe." Context reframing is seeing something in another context. For instance, a problem in one situation is actually a benefit in another. In the story, the burning hut is a problem in one context, but in another context it is a benefit because it saved the man's life!

So remember, the next time your hut is burning to the ground, instead of giving up hope and being consumed by the pain and suffering, reframe it, and give it context. Because what you think is a problem may actually be a smoke signal that God is placing in your life, you just haven't seen the benefit yet!

ACTION QUESTIONS

➔ **How can you use the concept of reframing to see things differently in your life?**

SET YOUR ANCHOR

Although I am not a sailor by nature, I know that anchoring is a very important part of any boating experience. You don't have to be in a boat for very long to realize that you can't stay in one place without throwing out your anchor.

If you do not anchor your boat, even on a calm day, the current will cause you to drift and you will find yourself in a place you had no intention of ending up. Once anchored, a boat will still move with the waves and current, however, it will remain stable and constant.

We need anchors in our lives as well. Without an anchor, we too will have a natural tendency to drift if we let the negative thoughts, emotions, adversity, and struggles of life take us away in their current. Remember, drifting is not caused by major things. It is caused by small, incremental currents of the sea that are not always visible to the eye. When you look on the surface, everything can seem normal and calm and the idea of drifting can easily be overlooked until it's too late, and you find yourself far away from where you planned.

And isn't that the same as life?

Everyday life will act the same way if we are not mentally strong and create a resilient mindset. Even though everything on the surface may seem normal, if we allow small, seemingly insignificant moments of fear or doubt or worry or negativity or excuses or procrastination to add up, then slowly but surely and without even knowing it, we will drift far away from our goals and dreams, not knowing how it happened.

So, what should you do instead?

SET YOUR ANCHOR.

There will always be something trying to pull up your anchor, like bad breaks, disappointments, setbacks, delays, and tough times. But instead you must set your anchor of positive energy. Rely on faith, gratefulness, love, and joy so that when life doesn't make sense and you are beginning to question the plan for your life...

you can set your anchor. When the vision for your life seems to be getting cloudy, distant, and out of reach... set your anchor. When you are starting to believe that the best thing to do is throw in the towel and give up...set your anchor.

Remember this: many of life's roughest storms are actually there to prove the strength of our anchors!

ACTION QUESTIONS

➜ **What is your anchor when things get tough?**

THE OTHER SIDE OF PRESSURE

Have you ever thought to yourself how some of the things we need most in life are made? Let's look at a few of them:

➔ Diamonds are formed at extremely high temperatures and under extreme pressure from the earth.

➔ Grapes have to be crushed in order to make wine.

➔ Olives must be pressed and worn down to be able to release their oils.

➔ Seeds grow in the darkness before they become food.

You are made the same way. At times, life can feel hard, stressful, and overwhelming. When it does, remember:

→ Whenever you feel the temperature rise...

→ Whenever you feel under extreme pressure...

→ Whenever you feel life is crushing you, pressing you, and wearing you down...

→ Whenever you feel yourself in a season of darkness...

Remember that you are not in a bad place, you are actually in a powerful place of transformation! Because all the things you want, desire, and need most in life are found on the other side of what you are currently going through.

Diamonds are one of the most precious and coveted items on the planet. When you look at how they are formed, most natural diamonds have an age of between 1 billion and 3.5 billion years and were formed in the earth's mantle at a depth between 150-250 kilometers below the surface. What makes them so expensive and rare is that so few diamonds are able to survive the difficult journey from the depths of the earth and to reach the earth's surface.

Just like the diamond, you must be resilient in the pursuit of what you desire. Resilience is the capability to withstand great difficulty and maintain the toughness to never give up. DO NOT GIVE UP. Whatever you are working towards and whatever you are going through, remember you are exactly where you need to be. You are in a powerful place of transformation and on the other side is where extraordinary happens!

ACTION QUESTIONS

→ **What is something you are willing to face extreme pressure for in order to get the results you want?**

HIDING UNDERWATER

"It is impossible to live without failing at something, unless you live so cautiously that you might as well not have lived at all. In which case, you fail by default."

J.K ROWLING

One of nature's amazing wonders is the iceberg! According to most estimates, about 10% of an iceberg is above water and the other 90% is below surface level. This means that when we look at an iceberg, we only get to see a fraction of the actual iceberg because most of its mass is hiding underwater. How we function as humans is very similar. What we think, how we feel, and the way we act is the 10% of human behavior that other people see of us. However, this behavior is driven by the 90% hiding under the surface, our core beliefs and story. The

90% hiding under your water level are the beliefs you have about why things are the way they are and the story you have told yourself over and over again about why things did or didn't work out in your life.

Have you ever failed at something?

Of course you have, we all have at some point in our lives. But the deeper question to ask is this: when you failed, why did you fail? The answer you give is a window into the 90% that lies within you. We all have a story about why we are where we are, and the story we tell protects us from the pain and suffering of why it isn't our fault. But the story protecting us is also the story that imprisons us because it keeps us from changing our life. Thus, our beliefs and story can either create barriers holding us back or be the platform that projects us to the next level in our future.

Author Joanne Kathleen Rowling is a wonderful example of how powerful the story we tell ourselves can be. According to Rowling: "By every usual standard, I was the biggest failure I knew."

Despite this, she went from living on welfare to being one of the world's wealthiest women. After she began writing the first Harry Potter novel, what followed was six tumultuous years of hardship. First losing her mother, then moving to Portugal and returning to England after a failed marriage and with a child. Jobless, penniless, and living on welfare, she received rejection after rejection from book publishers until finally one gave the green light for Harry Potter to be published...but under one request: she go by the name "J.K Rowling" since women's names were found to be less appealing. During this time, she could have quite easily created a story of blame and self-pity. Despite all the pain, loss, sorrow, and rejection she faced, J.K Rowling has gone on to sell over 400 million Harry Potter books and is worth an estimated $1 billion. And they said you could never make money being a writer!

When recalling her journey she said, "Failure meant a stripping away of the inessential. I stopped pretending to myself that I was anything other than what I was, and began to direct all my energy into finishing the only work that mattered to me."

If we are going to be successful, we are never going to get there by blaming others. Thus, we have to come up with a better story for our lives, a story that creates a call to action. If you are creative enough, determined enough, caring enough, bold enough, strong enough, and disciplined enough, you CAN find an answer to your problems!

Rewrite your story to one that will strengthen you, push you, and empower you to go beyond anything you have ever done in the past. Like the iceberg, your unlimited power lies hidden within you, waiting to surface and be shown to the world.

CHANGE YOUR STORY, CHANGE YOUR LIFE!

ACTION QUESTIONS

➜ **What is the story you must tell yourself that will change your life?**

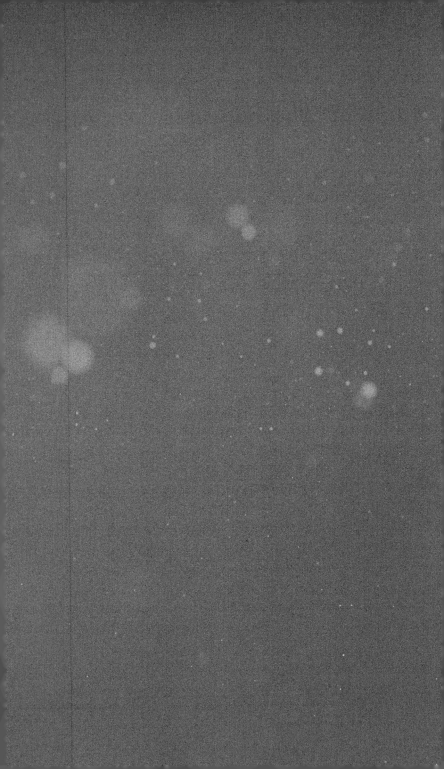

MAX MOMENTS ON HAPPINESS

SILVER MEDAL VS. BRONZE MEDAL

Have you ever dreamt about what it would be like to win an Olympic medal and be the best in the world at what you do?

Standing on the podium has to be a moment Olympians have always dreamt of. Yet when that moment finally arrives, for a certain few, the reaction is not quite what you would expect. For instance, you would assume a silver medalist would be just as happy, if not more, to be receiving their medal than the bronze medalist, right?

Not quite. Studies have shown bronze medalists to be much happier than silver medalists. Why?

The answer comes from a concept in psychology known as counterfactual thinking. This is basically the human tendency to create other possible alternatives to life events that have already happened. In the case of Olympians, it is imagining the outcome that didn't happen...

For the silver medalist, they are focused on what they didn't get, what they don't have, and how they just missed out on winning the gold medal, which creates a sense of unhappiness.

For the bronze medalist, they are focused on what they did get, what they do have, and how fortunate they are just to be on the podium, which creates a sense of happiness.

So, what is the lesson here? I am fascinated with how this same concept can also apply in our own lives. What type of lens do you view life through every day? What do you choose to focus on and how is it affecting your perspective on the events that happen in your life?

Do you find yourself getting caught up in "silver medal moments" thinking about all that is missing in your life, all that you don't have, and all that you haven't done. Just like the silver medalist who is comparing themselves to the gold medalist, maybe you are spending too much time comparing yourself to others around you and not enough time focused on your own personal development. If so, this may be affecting your ultimate happiness.

Instead, choosing to experience more "bronze medal moments" in your life like coming from a place of gratitude, focusing on all the blessings in your life, and what you have to be thankful for can significantly increase your happiness and sense of overall well-being.

Now don't get me wrong, just like you, I would much prefer to win the silver medal than the bronze medal (the gold medal would be even better!). But here is the truth...

Your happiness will never be found in having more of what you want, but rather in wanting more of what you have.

Motivational speaker Les Brown summed it up best when he said: "If you are not willing to risk you cannot grow, if you cannot grow you cannot become your best, if you cannot become your best you cannot be happy, and if you can't be happy then what else is there."

ACTION QUESTIONS

→ **What are some "silver medal moments" you have had that affected your happiness?**

→ **What are some "bronze medal moments" you can have that will increase your happiness?**

THE POSITIVITY RATIO

When you look inside what makes high-performing teams, high-performing cultures, or high performing relationships work, there are some key elements that drive this process. But there is one I want to share with you about the balance of positivity versus negativity.

Recent studies show that the communication of top performers is built on a very specific ratio of positive feedback, positive comments, and positive interactions to negative ones. One of the most important factors that can make the greatest difference in the efficiency, productivity, and the overall success of a team, a culture, a relationship, and a family is the ratio of our positivity to negativity.

Now before we go further, I want to make it clear that nothing is perfect. No relationship, no team, no culture is perfect, and you can't just be positive and happy all the time. That's not reality and studies are showing us we need both. We also need negative feedback because it can help us see our blind spots and areas of growth where we need to improve. It can also be a wake-up call, which we all need every now and again, and guard us against complacency, which can happen in the world of high performance.

Having said all that, negative feedback, negative comments, and negative interactions need to be balanced out with positive ones. So what is the MAGIC RATIO you ask?

That ratio is somewhere in the region of 5:1.

That means you need five positive interactions for every one negative one. Let me say this: The very best are using this formula to drive their performance.

Now, before we go any further, pause for a moment and ask yourself if you are currently working within that ratio, whether that is on your team, in the workplace, at home, or in your relationships. Are you honestly communicating and interacting with that equation? Be honest with yourself because pretending everything is ok won't help.

This is a moment to step back and see if this simple ratio can help improve your life.

For instance, one study showed that the difference between happy and unhappy marriages is this 5:1 ratio. They were able to predict with 90% accuracy whether couples would stay together or end up getting divorced based on their positivity versus negativity ratio!

Another study showed that the highest performing teams had an average positivity to negativity ratio of 5.6:1 (almost six positive interactions to one negative). The mediocre performing teams had an average ratio of 1.9:1 (almost twice as many positive interactions as negative ones). The lowest performing teams had an average ratio of 0.36:1 (almost three negative interactions for every positive one).

So let me say this again; as a top performer, high achiever, leader, captain, teammate, friend, wife, husband, daughter, son, or as someone who wants to make a greater impact in this world, what positivity ratio do you currently operate at? Are you unbalanced? If so, how can you create more positivity to help you get yourself and the people around you to the next level?

It was author Roy Bennett who said: "Attitude is a choice. Happiness is a choice. Optimism is a choice. Kindness is a choice. Giving is a choice. Respect is a choice. And whatever choice you make, makes you. Choose wisely."

I am saying the same to you: whatever Positivity Ratio you choose to make, makes you. Choose wisely!

ACTION QUESTIONS

→ **How would improving your positivity ratio help your performance and overall happiness?**

THE MAGNIFYING GLASS

The magnifying glass was originally invented in Europe around 1250. Fast forward to today and they come in hundreds of styles and sizes and are used for things ranging from home use all the way to scientific research.

For instance, a magnifying glass mounted in reading devices can magnify the reading print as much as ten times its normal size. Magnifying glasses can also be used in medical labs to magnify objects thousands of times, making it possible to see organisms that you would never normally be able to see. A magnifying glass is a powerful tool. What if we had the power to do the same thing and magnify images and emotions in our own life?

Imagine for a minute you have your own personal magnifying glass that you can use daily to intensify and elevate the most important things you want to focus and concentrate on...

What would you choose to magnify in your life?

Whatever you magnify in your life, you will feel with more intensity, and whatever you magnify in your life, you will elevate (sometimes with a magnification of 10X and up to 1000X stronger). Thus, it is very important to be conscious of what you use your magnifying glass for. Will it be what most people do, which is to magnify negativity, frustration, stress, fear, doubt, worry, sadness or excuses, and all the things that don't serve us well? Or will it be to magnify positivity, joy, love, appreciation, gratitude, faith, purpose, and possibility, and all things that will have a much greater impact on our happiness and how we lead our lives?

Look at it this way, your personal magnifying glass is going to increase your ability to see whatever it is you focus it on, but YOU are ultimately the one who gets to decide what you focus your magnifying glass on! The choice is yours...

ACTION QUESTIONS

Using your own personal magnifying glass:

➜ What do you want to magnify in your life?

➜ What do you want to reduce in your life?

THE SMILE EXPERIMENT

I believe that how we view life, the things we do in life, and what we are willing to go for in life largely comes down to how we SHOW UP in life. One of the biggest determining factors in how we show up to life is our ATTITUDE and ENERGY, because how you do anything is how you do everything.

One of the simplest ways to bring a positive attitude and positive energy to your day, and to bless others who you interact with, is with a smile! Make no mistake about it, a smile is a powerful thing. It is powerful because scientific studies have shown us that a simple smile can reduce levels of stress and increase levels of happiness. Now I know it doesn't take a scientific study to convince us about the benefits of smiling, but it is important that you understand this: we don't just smile because we are happy; we are happy because we smile. That is a very different way of looking at the power of a smile!

Did you know...

Children smile approximately 400 times per day.

And do you know how many times a day on average adults smile? 20.

So somewhere between childhood and adulthood, we have lost 380 smiles!

We have got to get those smiles back because of the power it can have on our day and the people around us.

So this is my challenge for you...

There is a term in human behavior called mirroring, which is when a person unconsciously imitates a gesture, speech, or attitude of another person in close proximity to them. Like when someone yawns close to you, you yawn as well! And just like yawning, smiling can be contagious too...So take the concept of mirroring, apply it to smiles.

There is one WARNING I have to add: Smiling more will make you happier, more attractive and more likable, so be ready!

ACTION QUESTIONS

→ How would your day be better if you smiled more?

→ Whose day would you make better if you smiled more?

→ How would your team's or organization's environment improve if you smiled more?

→ What mundane events or tasks would become more enjoyable if you smiled more?

THE MAIN THING AT THANKSGIVING

"Gratitude can transform common days into thanksgiving, turn routine jobs into joy, and change ordinary opportunities into blessings"

WILLIAM ARTHUR WARD

There is a powerful emotional state that is amplified every year during the holiday season at Thanksgiving. It is an emotion that fuels the essence and spirit of the holidays. Yet this same emotional state is something we don't have to wait until Thanksgiving for in order to enhance our health, happiness, and overall success. What I am talking about is the emotional state of gratitude.

Our lives are hectic. We fill our daily schedules with things we have to do, places we have to be, and deadlines we have to meet. With so many things to do, keeping what is most important at the forefront of our schedule can feel almost impossible. That is why it is so important, as Stephen Covey says: "To keep the main thing the main thing."

What if that main thing in your life was always gratitude and not just once a year at Thanksgiving? So much of our life is spent being worried, stressed, and fearful so gratitude takes an emotional back seat for the other 364 days of the year. But when you are grateful, there is no room for these other emotions. It is physiologically impossible to be grateful and fearful at the same time. When we are intentional about directing our focus toward all that we are thankful for, gratefulness, like a muscle, becomes stronger. Just like a muscle gains strength through being worked out repetitively, the emotion of gratitude strengthens within us when we repetitively choose to practice it.

When we focus on being GRATEFUL:

- ➔ We find all the things that are right in our life vs. finding all the things that are wrong in our life.

- ➔ We find all the things we have in our life vs. finding all the things we don't have in our life.

➤ We find all the ways to give of ourselves vs. finding all the ways to get for ourselves.

➤ We find all the best qualities in other people vs. finding all the worst qualities in other people.

The lenses through which you view life and all that happens to you will ultimately determine the quality of your life. There are many people in this world who seemingly have everything and they are miserable, and yet there are others who have faced extreme tragedy, have nothing, and are some of the happiest people on the planet. Why? Because problems and happiness have no relationship. You can have lots of problems in your life and still be happy just like you can have absolutely no problems and be totally unhappy. It all comes down to your perspective and what you focus on. FOCUS IS POWER and when you fix your eyes on being grateful, you begin to see your world and everything and everyone in it in a much different way. Unfortunately, most people will choose to focus on what's missing in their lives and miss out on many of life's beautiful gifts.

As Stephen Covey says, "The key is not to prioritize what's on your schedule, but to schedule your priorities."

I encourage you to make gratitude a daily priority and not just once a year for Thanksgiving. Consciously schedule time each day to give thanks and think about all the blessings in your life. When you're intentional with your thought process and gratefulness becomes a natural energy source, you will be emotionally rich!

ACTION QUESTIONS

➜ **How can you make GRATITUDE a daily priority in your life?**

AND THE WINNER IS...

"Every successful individual knows that his or her achievement depends on a community of persons working together."

PAUL RYAN

Who deserves the credit for your success?

If you said yourself then you are partly right, as we are all responsible for many of the decisions and choices we make leading to life's successes. However, it would be foolish of us to think that anyone could truly succeed purely on their own. I believe we all owe a debt of gratitude to the people that have had the biggest impact in our lives.

This idea of giving thanks to the most influential people in our lives is never more prominent than during "awards season" which runs from November through February. During this time, famous people gather for major galas such as the Golden Globes, Screen Actors Guild Awards, BRIT Awards, Grammy Awards, and every season ends with the most prestigious of them all, the Oscars! Customary at these awards ceremonies are the acceptance speeches that these actors, singers, producers, and directors have to make upon winning an award.

Those ninety seconds I find so fascinating because it is an opportunity for them to express their deepest thanks and appreciation for the special people that have helped them throughout their successful roles and careers. They know that achieving levels of greatness requires that we stand on the shoulders of giants and, when we do, we need to pay tribute to those who have had a lasting impact on our lives.

As Sir Isaac Newton pointed out, "If I have seen further, it is by standing on the shoulders of giants."

Now let me ask you: if you had ninety seconds to give your own acceptance speech, what would you say and whom would you thank for helping you get to where you are today?

Living with an attitude of gratitude is about feeling and expressing appreciation, and showing people how much we care about them is a big part of it. Thus, we must make a habit of telling those closest to us just how grateful we are for them.

I encourage you to be intentional about letting people know how much you appreciate them. Call and surprise someone you have not spoken to in a long time, write a letter or email, take someone out for lunch. It doesn't need to be elaborate, it just needs to come from your heart. Whoever that person is, be sure to let them know what value they have added to your life!

ACTION QUESTIONS

→ **If you had ninety seconds to give your own acceptance speech, what would you say and whom would you thank for helping you get to where you are today?**

THE CHINESE FARMER

There was an influential philosopher named Alan Watts who gave lectures at universities across the country. One favorite lesson was the story of the Chinese farmer...

Once upon a time there was a Chinese farmer whose horse ran away. That evening, all of his neighbors came around to commiserate with him, "We are so sorry to hear your horse has run away. This is most unfortunate."

The farmer said, "Maybe."

The next day the horse came back bringing seven wild horses with it, and in the evening everybody came back and said, "Oh, isn't that lucky. What a great turn of events. You now have eight horses!"

The farmer again said, "Maybe."

The following day, his son was riding one of the horses and he was thrown off and broke his leg. The neighbors then said, "Oh dear, that's too bad."

And the farmer responded, "Maybe."

The next day a group of officers came by to enroll people into the army, and they rejected his son because he had a broken leg. Again, all the neighbors came around and said, "Isn't that great!"

Again, he said, "Maybe."

Watts goes on to say: "The whole process of nature is an integrated process of immense complexity, and it's really impossible to tell whether anything that happens in it is good or bad. You never know what will be the consequence of the misfortune; or you never know what will be the consequences of good fortune."

You see, whatever happens in our life, we will never really know the consequences it may bring in the future. So it is important to come from a place where we view everything that happens to us as a gift. And I mean everything. The good and the bad, the highs and the lows, the wins and the losses, the successes and the failures, the things you want and the things you don't want. If everything in life is happening for us, that means the best is still yet to come, which gives us something to fight for each and every day!

ACTION QUESTIONS

→ **What does it mean when life is happening for you?**

→ **What does it mean when life is happening to you?**

CONNECT THE DOTS

Do you remember the coloring books where you would draw the lines to connect the dots?

When you first looked at the dots, sometimes it didn't make sense. But when you used the pencil to draw the lines and connected the dots, the picture became clearer and you could see much better.

Well, to me, those connect-the-dots coloring books are like life. You must connect the dots with all the events that happen in your life to be able to see clearly why things work out the way they do. Because if you take each event that happens in your life by itself, it may not make sense. When it doesn't, we can create a victim mindset: *poor me, why me, why do bad things always happen to me, how am I so unlucky, I guess it was not meant to be, maybe I don't deserve it,* the list goes on and on.

But when you connect the dots in your life by connecting one event that happens to another one you begin to see that there are patterns. You see things that you thought were negative in your life in a different way because they are connected to positive things. You start to see events, like setbacks, are actually a setup for something greater in your life. And when you connect the dots, you realize that you would not have been able to experience all the highest points in your life if it were not for some of the lowest points in your life.

Let me give you an example:

If I hadn't gotten cut from the soccer team I played for in England, I never would have made the biggest leap of faith in my life and moved to America...

If I hadn't moved to America, I never would have gotten into coaching...

If I hadn't gotten into coaching, I never would have met my beautiful wife...

If I hadn't met my beautiful wife, Life 2 The Max would not exist...

If I hadn't created Life 2 The Max, then I would not have written this book...

The fact I am sharing this message with you now means I am making my impact on the world doing what I feel I have been called to do.

That is how connected each event in my life has been. Yet if I had isolated the experience of getting cut when I was younger, then I could have defaulted to a victim mindset. But now I realize that by connecting the dots, what seemed to be one of the lowest points in my life is actually connected in creating the amazing life I live today. I am so grateful for that!

Think like you did when you were a child and connect the dots, it will change your life!

ACTION QUESTIONS

→ **What experiences in your life, if isolated look one way, but when connected have led to you experiencing some of the best moments in your life today?**

MAX MOMENTS ON THE JOURNEY

DESTINATION DISEASE

Take a moment and think about this question: What has to happen in order for you to consider yourself a success?

For many of us, we start by looking at a place called someday and begin thinking about what life might be like in the future when we can finally say "I made it". We view this place of success in the future as a DESTINATION we must arrive at in order to feel worthy enough to call ourselves successful. For example:

I will finally feel successful when:

- → Our team wins the championship

- → I become a starter and get more playing time

- → I meet the man/woman of my dreams or get married and start a family

➔ I am working at my dream job

➔ I get tons of followers and likes on social media

➔ I make lots of money, have a nice house and drive an expensive car

And the list goes on...

The problem is that this definition of success leads us toward a common illness known as "Destination Disease". This disease is often explained as arriving at your desired destination in life, at the place where you have always wanted to be, having everything you have always wanted to have, but when you finally get there you wonder... is this it?

When the destination becomes our obsession, it strips us of the very gift that makes achieving success worthwhile, which is the JOURNEY toward that destination. Thus, if the destination is the disease, then the journey is the cure! When the journey becomes our obsession, we instead allow ourselves the opportunity to fall in love with the process of living into our fullest potential and becoming all that we were designed to become. Henry David Thoreau explains this perfectly: "What you GET by achieving your goals is not as important as what you BECOME by achieving your goals"

Many Olympic athletes have been known to suffer from post-Olympic depression, a form of destination disease, after competing in arguably the pinnacle of their athletic careers. Athletes will spend years sacrificing so much for the opportunity to compete on the world's largest stage and, at the end, stand victorious on the podium with a gold medal around their neck. Upon arriving at their dream destination, the question for some is: Is this it?

For example, there is a part in the movie *Cool Runnings* where the coach of the Jamaican bobsled team is at the Winter Olympics talking to his team captain about his past as an Olympic athlete and what it means to win a gold medal. He explains that after winning a gold medal, he became so obsessed with winning and having to repeat this feat that he resorted to cheating in order to reach his desired destination. Upon reflection, he says: "A gold medal is a wonderful thing, but if you're not enough without it, you'll never be enough with it."

I want to remind you of this:

> ➤ If you are not enough without winning
> a championship, you will never be enough
> when you win it.

→ If you are not enough without being a starter on your team, you will never be enough when you are one.

→ If you are not enough without being in a relationship, you will never be enough when you are in one.

→ If you are not enough without having your dream job, you will never be enough when you have it.

→ If you are not enough without having lots of money, you will never be enough when you finally get it.

Your desired destination for success will never define you as a person, but the journey you undertake to get there will refine you into the person you will become. So, in your personal pursuit of success, I encourage you to trade your expectation for appreciation, trade what you want for what you have, trade the future for the present, and, finally, trade the DESTINATION for the JOURNEY...you won't regret it!

ACTION QUESTIONS

→ **What has to happen in order for you to consider yourself a success?**

THE LONGEST JOURNEY YOU WILL EVER TAKE

What is the longest journey you will ever take in your lifetime?

A trip to South Africa, Australia, Japan, Mount Everest, Hawaii...

For every trip you take, you can use a GPS system to map how to get there and get an exact overview of the route to take. But I would argue that the longest journey you will ever take in your lifetime is a place that cannot be found using a GPS system and does not come with an overview of how to get there. That journey is the 18 inches from your head to your heart!

The distance between your head and your heart, whilst only 18 inches, is the difference between information and transformation. With an unlimited amount of resources at our fingertips, we are drowning in information, yet we are starving for wisdom. Wisdom is the ability to think, process, and then act on all the information and knowledge that we have accumulated. In pursuit of our dreams and life purpose, we want the convenience of transformation without the inconvenience of what it will actually take to live out our very best life. So, why is it so hard for us to take this seemingly short 18-inch journey from our head to our heart?

Because of the unknown. To take the journey from your head to your heart, you have to be ok with stepping into the unknown. We would have no problem taking the journey if it was mapped out for us with an overview of how long it would take and the exact directions to follow. But the journey toward living our very best life doesn't give us that. We don't get a route overview of how it's going to happen, how long it's going to take, where the resources are going to come from and who we will meet along the way. Stepping into the unknown is hard, and it takes boldness.

When we make decisions from our head, we want all the information upfront before we take the journey.

When we make decisions from our heart, we use faith as the navigation system for the journey, which gives us the courage to step into the unknown. If you wait for all the information you think you need, you will be waiting your whole life!

When we make decisions from our head, we are looking for answers before we take the journey. When we make decisions from our heart, we are looking for reasons why we should take the journey. Reasons come first, answers come second. Remember, just because you don't have the answers does not mean you're not supposed to take the journey.

When we make decisions from our head, we ask the question: "Am I ready for the journey?"

When we make decisions from our heart, we ask the question: "Am I willing to take the journey?"

Let me be really honest with you. You will never be READY for the journey. You will never be ready for the amount of work you are going to have to put in, the insane focus it is going to take, what you are going to have to walk away from, all the people who are going to doubt you, not to mention the sacrifice, struggle and suffering you will have to endure before you succeed.

But rather you must ask yourself, are you WILLING? Are you willing to put in the time and effort that is required, are you willing to get let down, are you willing to be doubted, are you willing to face disappointment, are you willing to pick yourself back up when you get knocked down, are you willing to sacrifice things, are you willing to leave the people behind that are holding you back, are you willing to face all the adversity coming your way and keep going. Are you willing to take a leap of faith into the unknown?

Maybe the reason we don't know about our future and have to step into the unknown is because if we saw how difficult it is going to be to achieve what we are truly capable of, we might talk ourselves out of it and never achieve all that we were made for.

SO...

- ➜ When would NOW be a good time to start?

- ➜ When would NOW be a good time to move from information into transformation?

- ➜ When would NOW be a good time to take one of the longest but most rewarding journeys of your life, the 18 inches from your head to your heart?

ACTION QUESTIONS

➜ It's your NOW or NEVER moment. Are you willing to take it?

REFERENCE SECTION

Homing Instinct

https://www.allaboutbirds.org/news/the-basics-migration-navigation/#

https://www.goodreads.com/quotes/7495222-another-statistical-survey-of-7-948-students-at-forty-eight-colleges-was

One Marshmallow or Two

https://en.wikipedia.org/wiki/Stanford_marshmallow_experiment

10 Seconds of Courage

chrome-extension://efaidnbmnnnibpcajpcglclefindmkaj/https://sciendo.com/pdf/10.2478/bhk-2013-0018

Silver Medal vs. Bronze Medal

https://time.com/6145596/2022-winter-olympics-bronze-silver-medals-happiness/

The Positivity Ratio

https://www.inc.com/jessica-stillman/use-magic-51-ratio-to-improve-all-your-relationships.html

https://hbr.org/2013/03/the-ideal-praise-to-criticism

The Smile Experiment

https://www.nbcnews.com/better/health/smiling-can-trick-your-brain-happiness-boost-your-health-ncna822591

MORE OPPORTUNITIES TO LIVE LIFE 2 THE MAX!

TO LEARN MORE...

For additional resources including
coaching programs, events and speaking opportunities,
scan the QR code below or visit www.maxrooke.com

TO CONTACT MAX DIRECTLY...

Email: LiveL2TM@gmail.com
Twitter: @Max_Rooke
Instagram: @maxjrooke
YouTube: @Max_Rooke
Facebook: Life2TheMax
LinkedIn: maxrooke